FOREIGN AID AND FOREIGN POLICY

FOREIGN AID
and FOREIGN POLICY

Herbert Feis

St Martin's Press	New York
Macmillan & Co. Ltd.	London
Macmillan of Canada	Toronto

SECOND PRINTING

Copyright © 1964 by Herbert Feis
All Rights Reserved
Library of Congress Catalog Card Number: 64–18364
Manufactured in the United States of America by H. Wolff, New York

Preface

American views and the international outlook have veered since I started this study of the vibrating connections between foreign aid and foreign policy.

A few years ago prevalent American opinion, popular and professional, was assured about the value of foreign aid as a complement to American foreign policy and strategy. Now the tenor of national judgment is downcast and doubtful.

At that time the American government while reaching out to assist all poor and emerging countries, relied on their professions of good intentions. It was not thought advisable or necessary to make explicit stipulations for recipients of aid to observe. More recently the official attitude has become mistrustful and exigent.

Then there was an almost unchallenged acceptance of the prospect that the cold war would continue without relaxation against the whole Communist world. In the interval fissures have appeared in that seemingly unified front. A belief is emerging that American diplomacy may prudently strive to reach a basis for peaceful cooperation with such Communist countries as genuinely seek it. This view should be reflected in the conduct of the American programs of foreign aid if the trend of peaceful cooperation continues.

Not long since, the United States was ardently weaving alliances with the many small states of Asia, Africa and the Middle East. Our policy assumed that proffers of economic assistance would be a convincing token of our wish to see these states grow strong and prosper; and that they, in appreciation, would return our friendship. Now, many Americans are in a state of mild shock at the unruly conduct and quarrelsomeness of many of these countries. In consequence the United States may possibly retreat from its responsibilities in some of these areas, unless their ways and attitude recommend them more than they do at present.

Then there was a great spurt of hope for the quick realization of the fine and humane ends of the Alliance for Progress. But since that Alliance was inaugurated, hopes have slowed and quieted down because many of the Latin American countries have been managing their economic, political and social affairs so poorly. And a few seem to be trying to prove their national virility by a display of contempt for American aid. The belief that, stimulated by American encouragement and aid, they would make the efforts and reforms essential for material progress which would ultimately sustain itself has come into question.

This book has been written in a period of rapid change. It is presented with the hope that its historical perspective and analytical comments will steady American foreign aid policy in the face of such vicissitudes and surprises of international life.

Another thought kept me engaged in the task. There is still a genuine need to mesh more closely the problems of attaining material improvement and those arising in the attempt to use foreign aid as an agent of foreign policy. I have tried to indicate how the competence displayed in each of these fields affects the other; and why and how, therefore, diplomats must be economic judges and economists must be political prophets.

I wish to thank the Rockefeller Foundation for the grant which enabled me to carry out the task; and Columbia University for administering the grant; and the Brookings Institute for giving me an office in which, at the start of my study, I could acquaint myself with the pertinent literature; and the Institute for Ad-

vanced Study at Princeton for again appointing me to membership and providing me with a pleasant place to work and with
secretarial help; and the staffs of the libraries of Princeton University and the Council on Foreign Relations for their generous and
intelligent help, which I have come to expect of all American libraries and librarians; and Mrs. Lari Ault and Mrs. Virginia M.
Rowe for their stalwart and patient performance of the wearisome
task of typing and checking the many versions of the manuscript.

To my wife, Ruth Stanley-Brown Feis, my loving gratitude
for sustaining my effort in every way, and then undaunted, reading the proofs and preparing the Index.

Some of the ideas contained in this study were first presented in
lectures given under the auspices of the Department of State in
several universities of France and Greece. Chapters were used
in lectures at Occidental College in California, and to my hosts
there I wish to convey my appreciation.

Herbert Feis
York, Maine
1963

In the brief interval between the original edition and this
slightly revised version of my essay, the ways of the nations have
not changed—much—either for better or worse. Nor have the relations between the great powers and the state of the cold war,
though both may be in flux. Thus it has not seemed to me to be
necessary to make substantial revisions in the text. But I have introduced some new factual information about recent events and
experiences in further illustration of my observations.

Regrettably, the protracted arguments in Congress over the current Foreign Assistance Act revealed a still further ebbing of faith
in the program. This is indicated not only by reduction of the
sums allocated, but also by the introduction of some more stringent
stipulations to which the extension of aid is made subject.

H. F. York, Maine 1964

Contents

Part one |

THE HISTORICAL AURA

1 | Toward the Subject

Thirty years or so ago in a book called *Europe: the World's Banker: 1870–1914,* I tried to trace the interplaits between the large British, French and German foreign investments and the foreign policy of these three powers during this era. In retrospect the task appears easy.

The dispensers of foreign loans and investments were private capitalists all. The incentives and purposes which governed their activities were plain. The providers of capital sought a larger return than could be had at home, plus the presumed safety of diversifying assets. Their governments wanted them to prosper and the return flow of income from abroad to grow. Believing that this overflow of financial power would serve foreign policy, each of these three governments tried to ensure that it would do so.

The main features and facts had been exposed to the scholar. Almost all the larger financial transactions were of public record. The history of the discussions and negotiations preceding most arrangements had been revealed. In the aftermath of the First World War and the Russian Revolution the diplomatic archives had been flung open. During the subsequent years the British, German and French governments had published the official documentation of their diplomacy. Thus the student could find full and reliable information about why, how and when the governments of three lending countries acted as watchers and wardens of the foreign ventures of their citizens.

Moreover, in the nineteen-twenties men still believed that the world was orderly and dependable. Despite the Bolshevik convulsion and shocking disturbances elsewhere, historical interpretation and judgment could still rest on the assumption that the basic political and social pattern of Europe and the Western hemisphere would continue much the same as before the war; as would the balance of importance, economic, political and military, between the more remote countries and the Western world. When I wrote, it was not yet recognized how deep was the damage wrought by the war, how frail the peace settlements, how fierce and many the lingering hatreds.

The world in which I take up the theme again in this book is different in its fibers, forms and forces. Of what was, and what has gone and what is left of the earlier one, many other historians have told and will continue to tell.

The transactions embraced in the current concepts and practices of "foreign aid" are of various kinds. In this inquiry, our attention will be confined to one—to those activities and engagements in which means are provided explicitly for economic and attendant social purposes.

In the thirty-year interval the nature of these activities and engagements has changed in three important ways. The predominant private foreign investment is different in character. Governments, especially the American government, have become the chief supplier of technical advice and capital to the really poor countries. Multinational agencies are being endowed with much larger funds and used much more extensively.

In the earlier period most privately owned investment in foreign countries consisted of bonds purchased of foreign governments and the stocks and bonds of private foreign companies. This kind of investment is known as "portfolio" investment. Recently private capitalists in the United States have resumed this activity, gov-

erned by the same pecuniary reckoning as before. But more important now is "direct" investment by American (and Western European) industrial organizations in foreign subsidiaries which they
own and operate. That diffusion of private enterprise has been
rapid and cumulative. However, most such direct investment by
industrial firms has gone into countries that are well advanced
economically and within a familiar political orbit. True, great
sums have been provided for ventures in the extractive industries,
particularly oil and metal mining, in countries and areas otherwise
offering little or no inducement to foreign private capital—particularly in the Arab states of the Middle East and in Venezuela. But
otherwise little such industrial capital has been attracted into the
poorest, neediest countries, whose people are not qualified to operate modern factories and whose purchasing power is small. It
has stayed out of areas where the prospect of profit was poor compared to the risks, as it is in many essential public service industries.

But it is in these impoverished countries, and in these essential
public service industries, that the need for help is greatest. Since
it was determined that this need could or should not be ignored,
governments, led by the American government, stepped forward
to "aid" countries and projects which private capital would not or
could not finance. These "suppliers" of aid have broader incentives
than have private capitalists and different standards of decision.[1]

These changes, compounding one another, have made it much
harder to know what is going on, and to judge the meaning and
consequences of foreign aid activities. My efforts to grasp, as one
year gave in to the next, what part the provision of foreign aid was

---

1. I have not been able to find or make up a portmanteau word, the meaning of which would properly contain and convey the various roles played by
countries that supply capital and other kinds of help; keepers of arsenals and
distributors of weapons, trainers of armed forces, donors, lenders, investors,
bargainers. For the sake of brevity I shall use the neutral word "supplier" to
denote the country providing any kind of aid. Similarly, I have used the word
"recipient" to denote a country that receives any kind of aid from others.

playing in American foreign policy and what part foreign policy was playing in it, usually left my thoughts in confusion. My reading of the extensive Hearings before Committees of the Senate and the House of Representatives, and of the abounding books and articles on the subject, left the impression that I had much company in my groping. Clearly, also, a review of the record revealed how often since first the American government engaged in extending foreign aid it has changed its views as to how this power should and could be used to serve foreign policy. The world, in all salient aspects, has been in flux. Experience has been a rude teacher, forcing the authorities to revise their ideas and methods.

My perplexities impelled me to seek a clarifying arrangement of thoughts about this realm of activity. All that this long essay pretends to be is an attempt to elucidate the main elements and links. It is an assembly of historical notes and interpretations and aphorisms. These may help to locate American efforts in perspective, and explain them in the clutch of uncontrolled turmoil. The range of my comment being so wide and its purport being inconclusive, it can do no more than enlist judgment and appeal for agreement.

As my study proceeded, a parable formed in my mind around the vicissitudes of Captain Cook on one of his voyages of exploration along the coasts of New Zealand. On one side of the peninsula where Auckland now stands, he and his companions were well received by the natives, the Maoris. They provided his men and ship with food and supplies, and sought instruction from the visitors in the use of some of the simpler gear and tools. This anchorage the Captain named the Bay of Plenty. On the opposite side of the peninsula the natives repelled his advances, refused to provide any supplies, and rejected gifts. This anchorage he named Poverty Bay.

The two are still called by these names. But hardworking and frugal men and women from far away settled along both bays; better methods of production were learned and practiced; foreign capital was attracted; the people and government worked together spontaneously, and now both are thriving.

And as my study became enveloped in the difficulties of helping others, and in the dilemmas met, one change wrought by foreign aid became a banner or pennant for the struggle against pervasive poverty. Along the short stretch of shore in Southeast Australia, called Botany Bay, the once desolate locale of the first convict settlements, there now stands a huge American-owned oil refinery, source of energy for a free and flourishing continent.

The commentator on present American ventures in foreign economic aid is made cautious by his collisions with the unexpected in the record of the past. He notes how often our foreign policies have had an aberrant outcome. He recalls that during the thirties, in an effort to insulate the United States against strife in Europe, the American government did almost nothing to strengthen or support the opponents of the Axis: and then was forced to recognize that its aloofness had imperiled our own future. He recollects how steadfastly the United States supported China, first against the European governments which were bent on dividing it into spheres of influence, and then against Japan; yet, our ward, China, was transformed into an enemy. Still alive is our assumption that the profusion of American economic activities in Cuba benefited all its people, and that they looked up to us and regarded us as friends; and our astonishment at finding out that extremist leaders could win support in assaults on everything American. And just on the edge of memory are the perplexities presented to the American government by the conduct of the Diem-Nhu regime in Vietnam, which it had so stubbornly upheld and generously financed—till approval turned into critical disapprobation.

Or, to recall a most important instance in which the outcome was better than the expectation: our belated recognition after the war that we had to help our former European allies to combat the forces of Communism within and without; and our pleased surprise at their rapid revival of production and political vitality.

Who, in 1948—when the Marshall Plan was started—forecast that fifteen years later these distressed and divided countries would be reproved by the American government because they were not sharing their great prosperity enough with poorer countries?

Little wonder then that most Americans have been becoming more and more aware of the surprising mutability of the foreign societies which they set out to support and assist to emerge from poverty.

The hazards of foresight will probably be as great in the future as in the past, and the stumbles as painful. But the chance that even the best laid plans for helping others may go awry should not cause us to shirk our self-assumed responsibility or to become fatalists. It should be, rather, a stimulus to harder thought and more thorough scrutiny of the facts we face.

In this field decisions must remain only informed guesses as to how the countries we nurture will conduct themselves. Their response, as the years pass, will be a swirling compound. It will be, in incessantly varying proportions, respect, gratitude, liking, indifference, suspicion, greed, envy, pride and caprice. Hope of future favors may count more than favors already received, except between countries firmly associated with each other or in common peril. In other words, ventures in foreign aid are plunges into the depths of national behavior. The investigator of their course must pursue them through the tangle of tendencies and tensions that bend under uncharted local and international tides and currents.

2 | Toward the Theory of
Material Improvement

As John Maynard Keynes observed, "The belief in the material progress of mankind is not old. During the greater part of history such a belief was neither compatible with experience nor encouraged by religion." But since those early nineteenth century treatises that caused economics to be called the "dismal science" were written, the prevailing hue of judgment about the prospects of improving the lot of most of mankind has changed from dark to light—or rainbow colored.

Economists and other informed students now incline toward the conclusion that cumulative economic growth is attainable by all countries. Until not long ago, in fact, they seemed to regard it as assured. But recent pauses and setbacks have caused them to become more cognizant of the many obstacles to economic progress. This clash between potentiality and actuality may be made clear by tracing, briefly and selectively, the evolution of presently prevailing ideas.

Unrivaled in authority up to the great depression was the analysis of the operation of the economies of the Western world known as the "classical" theory. Embedded in its confined abstractions the outlines of a theory of economic growth may be found. The basic elements are few and simple. Growth—material progress— is made possible by toil, thrift, and trade. A people could climb out of poverty to ease by working hard, saving, and permitting competitive trade within the country and with other countries. Their analysis allowed for the fact that countries with superior natural resources would find it easier to progress than those whose resources were scanty.

Toil, the earnest use of the powers of body and mind, was the creating constituent of production. The greater and more pro- longed the effort, the more copious the product might be, though the reward of those who did the work might not always grow correspondingly.

Thrift was the progenitor of capital. It enabled those who saved their income to hire labor and natural resources—to construct factories, to make and use tools and machines, to build roads, railways and ships, to clear land and raise crops and herds, to buy and process raw materials. Thus physical capital was the generator of employment and higher productivity; especially so, since it brought about the division and specialization of labor. Moreover, capital gave the spirit of enterprise greater realm and reach; and the spirit of enterprise found and made better and larger chances for capital.

Trade between countries was the way in which this division and specialization of effort was made world-wide. For each coun- try would be induced and enabled to procure from others those goods which it could not produce itself, or could produce only at much greater real cost.

But the prospect of material progress as disclosed in these classi- cal theories was so hedged round by fearful imperatives that the vista of material progress for the many as well as the few was left in obscure doubt. Results would match possibilities only if presumed tendencies commonly called "economic laws" were re- spected. Each and all must be permitted to engage in the opera- tions which seemed most promising to them and to invest their capital as they wished. Supply and demand must be allowed to set prices and wages and determine the distribution of income. Even then, the condition of the workers on farms, in factories, mines, ships, and offices could not be bettered if their numbers grew faster than the supply of good natural resources and the accretion of capital. Only on these terms could growth be attained and poverty relieved.

The classical theoreticians bequeathed clear and sound identification of the chief nutrients of growth to the present. But they reasoned that the defects of the operation of unregulated economic activity were transient and self-correcting. They deprecated social ideals and personal inclinations that interfered with the operation of what they conceived to be primary economic laws. They slighted the effect which advancing technology would have upon prospects of material improvement.

The interest of the formulators of the classical theory centered on the position, problems and policies of Western Europe, especially of Great Britain. The institutions and attitudes which prevailed in that region—and in those parts of the New World to which its people and capital were migrating—formed their suppositions and shaped their conclusions. Yet this set of doctrines and rules was deemed by disciples to be of universal validity; to mark the path of progress for all countries, communities and climates.

Hence it was assumed that the private foreign investment from the richer capitalist countries would benefit the poorer or less developed lands into which it flowed, provided that the requisite terms were met and the ways and rules of good economic conduct were observed.

During the same decades in which the classical theory had most influence, a set of doctrines—Socialist-Communist ones—were developed that challenged its analysis, denied its conclusions, and scorned its standards. While the classical theory absolved private capital from censure for lack of progress unless its conditions and terms were met, this critical creed blamed it for the plight of all who were poor and miserable.

The amalgam of historical criticism, abstract theory, prophecies and revolutionary appeals which make up the Socialist-Communist doctrines of economic life and society was given its impacting form in the writings of Marx and Engels about a century ago. Even in their original presentation, these doctrines were incoherent. Since then they have been densely overgrown by the tendrils of thought spun by disciples and commentators. Today, believers must accept whatever version is taught by those who teach them or control their careers, and renounce it when they are charged with being "deviationists." Thus any interpreter must expect to be accused of mistaking false doctrine for the one and only correct one.

This compound won attention because of its intellectual vigor and its arousing moral tone. Its intrinsic ambiguity has favored rather than hindered its diffusion. For in its dense substance, all who are living in poverty, who are overworked, and the failures, and all who are disaffected with the ways and results of capitalism, can find some item of truth and some just emotional satisfaction. Each and every one can construe the prescription for a regenerated society to suit his need or wishes. In short, the Marxian-Engels-Leninist-Stalinist-Mao-tse Tung texts and precepts contain the same brew of elements as do most other religions: probing insights into human nature and society, over-all obscurity of meaning, vividness of image; moral indignation that can justify indulgence in scorn, hatred and cruelty, and a vision of a better and more just future. Thus, allegiance to these doctrines cannot be dispelled merely by disproving the accuracy or balance of its historical tales, or by showing up their distortions of perspective, or by dissecting the logic of their technical analysis.

We need take note only of the import of the Marxian presentation for the problems of economic development and growth, especially of the poorer countries. It stems from the same bases as the classical theory. In both, process of productivity is viewed as the application of human labor to natural resources with capital as the active intermediary. In both exists a kindred belief that the amount of amassed capital determines the rate of economic activity and the level of productivity. But otherwise the Marxian reasoning diverged vitally from the classical in its judgment of prospects for material progress under the capitalist system.

In the classical doctrine it was assumed that all savings would be invested for further gain. As succinctly expressed by Adam Smith: "What is annually saved is as regularly consumed as what is annually spent . . . but it is consumed by a different set of people." Thus, it was concluded that the accumulation of capital without end could—and presumably would—add without limit to the production and wealth of a people. It would bring opulence to some, and if their numbers did not grow too fast, betterment to all. But in the Marxian portrayal of the inner tendencies of capitalism, it is contended that the amount of capital amassed by the owners of the means of production will outrun profitable opportunities; and that this will cause economic stagnation and distress, plunging society into recurrent and worsening crises of overproduction. Industrial workers would never earn more than the minimum pay needed to enable them barely to subsist and serve. Peasants and farm laborers similarly were condemned to life-long servitude and poverty by oppressive landlords and money lenders. These tendencies, it was predicted, would eventually bring about the collapse of the capitalist system, when the workers, roused to revolt by their misery, seized control of the government and took possession of the means of production. Then under Communist direction, growth could start.

Consistently the expositors of Marxist doctrines averred that the flow of private capital into foreign lands was compulsive, caused by the need to employ surplus capital and to dispose of surplus commodities. In their texts foreign investment is scored as a frantic attempt by the capitalists to stave off depression and save themselves. The poor and weak countries, Communist dogma preaches, will not be helped by foreign capital to become better off and stronger. Instead, their workers would be exploited, their natural resources would be stolen, and they would be reduced to subjection. These accusations were hurled not only against the foreign private capitalists but also against the governments which were held to be at times merely the servant, at times the abettors, of the capitalists. Both were condemned as being indifferent to the welfare of the local inhabitants of the countries into which capital and commerce penetrated.

During the decades when these interpretations were being absorbed by the men who were to become the insurgent leaders of Socialist and Communist revolutions, they were made plausible by some of the actions of Western capitalist groups and governments. It was the second great era of spreading colonialism and struggle for empire—an era which reached its woeful climax in the First World War.

Yet, despite the shattering effects of that war, Western communities rejected Communist dogma as false and repugnant. They clung to their basic attitudes and their belief in the possibilities of material improvement under capitalism. But the times called for new presentations of the route to growth that would have the restorative force that the classical theory had lost. They were needed to energize depressed peoples and economies. The challenge evoked a lively response. During the decades between the two great world wars several corrective analyses of the processes and possibilities of the capitalist system of production emerged. They offered invigorating remedies for economic recovery and progress.

One type of presentation became known as the Technocratic theory. Its authors and proponents tried to leap over or bypass the intricacies, economic and social, of the processes of production and distribution of income which had engrossed the attention of both the classical economists and the Communist critics.

Their thought was not intellectually novel. What made it striking was the will to demonstrate how much growth was attainable if a society strove hard for it, and lessened wastes and frictions. They assumed that the current system of production and the nature of the current flow of internal exchange of goods and services would not change much. They focused their statistical studies upon estimates of what *could* be produced by existing human effort and talent, natural resources, technical knowledge and machines.

The Technocrats—statisticians—engineers—managers—thought their tabulated conclusions established the fact that if all these assets were fully and well used, the resultant supply of goods and services would be so ample that all contributors to production could live much better. No less appealing was their inference that nations would then not need to contend against one another for trade and investment chances, and that the richer nations could help the poorer without controlling their affairs. It was taken for granted that if peoples were aroused by this vision of plenty, they would be able in one way or another to accumulate the capital needed to effectuate the technological revolution.

These examiners proceeded from estimates of what could be done with existing means and knowledge to forecasts of how much more could be done as new advances in technology led to leaping increases in productivity. Invention (to use this one familiar word to represent all sorts of new physical means, methods, processes of production and products), they deposed, could enlarge real income in two ways: first by enabling capitalists, managers and workers to produce more or better goods with the same exertion and capital; second by stimulating competition since all who want to win must be more alert and bold. The theory of the processes of growth under capitalism that seeped out of these studies of technical capabilities was succinctly stated by Joseph Schumpeter in his provocative study:

> Economic progress . . . means turmoil. . . . Possibilities of gain to be reached by producing new things or by producing old things more cheaply are constantly materializing and calling for new investments. . . . This is how "progress" comes about in

capitalist society. In order to escape being undersold, every firm is in the end compelled . . . to invest in its turn, and in order to be able to do so, to plow back part of its profits i.e. to accumulate. Thus, everyone else accumulates.[1]

When first diffused the hopeful calculations of the Technocrats aroused only a passing flurry in the Western industrialized nations. Paradoxically, they made a greater impress on the minds of the rulers of the Soviet Union, who hailed them as proof of the defects of capitalism, and thus as justification for the Soviet system of production based on a total plan with power to compel all to conform to its requirements.

Now, irrespective of their form of economic society, almost all nations are converts to the faith in the transforming power of technology. The impersonal vitamin of growth is highly prized and sought after.

To those countries trailing in their economic performance, this simple and assured vista of growth is most alluring. For almost the whole lexicon of technical knowledge is now open to them. The leading industrial countries no longer wait for those seeking information about means, methods and processes of production to come to them. They purvey it through books and articles. They display and demonstrate new inventions at fairs. They hunt for purchasers of industrial licenses and patent rights. They send out consultants and specialists with samples. When needy countries cannot afford to pay for this technical assistance, more affluent ones provide it on credit or free. In short, it can almost be said that those capitalist countries that are advanced in technical fields, particularly the United States, beseech others to buy, borrow, beg or steal their ways of production and their products.

While the Technocrats were dramatizing the span between actual and attainable production, John Maynard Keynes was subjecting the operations of the capitalist system to a severe inspec-

1. Joseph A. Schumpeter, *Capitalism, Socialism and Democracy*, page 32.

tion. His quest was purposeful. Why was production and employment so often, and for so long a period, so much less than it could be? What interests and propensities were responsible? Or what faults of understanding or errors of policy? He went in search of the causes of trouble and when he thought he had located them, sought the remedies.

Keynes concluded that the capitalist system, unguided, could not be relied on to display the dynamic qualities extolled in that brief excerpt from Schumpeter just quoted. He detected propensities which he thought would prevent the ingredients of growth stressed in classical doctrine from carrying the economy forward. Unless offset these would, he argued, continue to bring on slumps and stagnation as they had periodically in the past. While thus rebelling against the dictates of older theory, he strove to find correctives which would enable countries to assure themselves of steady progress as their capital grew and their technical knowledge advanced. He believed he found them, and that if the indicated measures were vigorously used, the heights glimpsed by the Technocrats could be easily reached without direct compulsion.

To extract or deduce from the Keynesian analyses their meaning in regard to problems of economic growth is not easy. Keynes' judgment on certain major issues of theory and fact, sometimes flung out hastily from different angles of observation and interest, were not always fused or coordinated. Contradictions lurk in the folds of his explanations.

One of Keynes' observations was akin to that in the Marxian doctrine: that there was a tendency in the system of private enterprise, as then operative, for savings to pile up at times in uninvested hoards. In this he thought he detected the main cause of slumps. However, he rejected the sequential conclusion of Communist theorists that this tendency *must* lead to cascading crises. He confirmed the traditional view that the cumulative increase in savings was an essential enabling element of growth. What had to be done, and this above all else, he insisted, was to see that all savings or their equivalent, were promptly employed as productive capital. The general tenor of his thought on this question was, perhaps, most succinctly conveyed in his comment on the so-called "oversaving" or "underconsumption" theories of European and American economists—dissenters but not Communists. "Insofar," Keynes wrote in 1933, "however, as these theories maintain that the existing distribution of wealth tends to too large a volume of savings, which leads in turn to over-investment, which leads to too large a production of consumption-goods, they are occupying a different terrain from my theory; inasmuch as, in my theory, it is a large volume of saving which does *not* lead to a correspondingly large volume of investment (not one which *does*) which is the root of the trouble." [2]

This being so, he advocated that it should be public policy to see that all savings be put to quick use. This, he argued, called for bold directness. Much more than had been done could be done by more vigorous use of the familiar battery of monetary, banking and fiscal measures. But as he continued to mull over the problem, he became dubious whether these would suffice. The trend of his further thought is indicated by his profession that, "For my own part I am now somewhat skeptical of the success of a merely monetary policy directed towards influencing the rate of interest. I expect to see the State, which is in a position to calculate the marginal efficiency of capital goods on long views and the basis of its general social advantage, taking an ever greater responsibility for directly organizing investment. . . ." [3]

One reason why his writings, though caustically critical of the conventional ideas and practices of businessmen, bankers and politicians, were read with such respectful interest was because they were animated by a wish to preserve the main traditional ways and forms of Western society. Another was because they conveyed buoyant assurance that by a proper combination of private activities and public initiative all peoples of the world could

2. *A Treatise on Money,* Volume I, page 179, italics in Keynes' text.
3. *The General Theory of Employment, Interest and Money,* page 164.

progress toward a far better material future. Thus, in a statement of faith, he had written in 1930: "All this means in the long run *that mankind is solving its economic problem.* I would predict that the standard of life in progressive countries one hundred years hence will be four to eight times as high as it is today," and "I draw the conclusion that, assuming no important wars and no important increase in population, the *economic problem* may be solved or at least within sight of solution within a hundred years. This means that the economic problem is not—if we look into the future—the *permanent problem of the human race.*" [4]

Keynes' insistence that all savings must be invested was transformed by disciples into a formula—almost a panacea—for assuring economic growth. What had to be done was to see to it that investment in creative production was equal to, or greater than, the current volume of savings. When private investment was not sufficient to keep the productive system fully employed, it should be supplemented by government initiative. This was turned by the more ardent disciples into a rule which would enable any country to surmount circumstances and overcome its deficiencies.

Actually Keynes' concern was focused on the plight and problems of the few advanced industrial countries, especially Great Britain, as had been that of the classical economists. His general analyses are structured upon their national systems and situations. His reflections on the affairs and prospects of the many very poor and undeveloped countries were incidental to his primary intent, and were usually tossed off in short essays.

Even so, what he wrote has had a strong and mounting influence on attitudes about the problems of material improvement everywhere. Some followers were the more attracted by the substrata of meaning in his reproaches of the capitalist system for not living up to its promises, others by the affirmativeness of his

4. Italics in Keynes' text. This essay on the *Economic Possibilities for Our Grandchildren* was reprinted in *Essays in Persuasion.* However, the first sentence of the Preface which Keynes wrote in 1930 for this volume is "Here are collected the croakings of twelve years—the croakings of a Cassandra who could never influence the course of events in time."

recommendations. Out of these two there formed into the mind of students in every corner of the world a conviction that their country could improve its material condition.

This faith in the procreative power of invested capital pervades many of the most widely read recent books on the problems of assistance to poorer countries.[5] The worshipful expositors of the magic of capital do not deny that in the past the progress of technology has been the germinal cause of greater productivity. But they stress that technical mastery of problems of production is now adequate to enable countries to better themselves—if they can save or get the capital needed to take advantage of it. As epitomized in one of Barbara Ward's statements, "If technology is the key to producing more output with less use of resources—productivity—then capital—or saving—is the only key to technology. Without saving there is no economic growth." [6]

This manner of statement obscures the dynamics of growth. The connection between the volume of saving and rate of growth is involuted and vibrating.

Moreover, in many of the poorer countries where there is an ample labor supply superior methods of doing a job need no more capital than did the poorer ones they supersede. Proven examples abound; as in the hauling of heavy loads uphill, the weaving of stronger fishing nets, the building of the walls of a village house, the stripping of bamboo for outer cover or thatch, the raising of healthier livestock or the growing of selected or better seeds. But even when this is the case—when no more capital may be required to use labor and resources in better ways—in order to do so more tools, machines, parts, materials, technical advisers, may have to

5. As for examples, that of Ragnar Nurske's *Problems of Capital Formation in Underdeveloped Countries,* and the voluminous studies written by the group at Massachusetts Institute of Technology of which those of Max Millikan and Walt W. Rostow aroused the greatest interest, and the eloquent articles and lectures of Barbara Ward, as in her recent book *The Rich and Poor Nations.*

6. Barbara Ward, *ibid.,* page 96.

be imported. Hence the poorer countries must secure more external purchasing power by trade or aid.

A few planners and advocates during the past decade have become bold enough to try to formulate a general rule or law of dosages of capital required to prime and sustain economic growth. Their consensus has tended to the conclusion that if and as a country saves and productively invests 12 to 15 per cent of its gross national income year after year, it should soon be able to achieve continuous growth *without outside help*. Some of the calculators support their estimates by imputed historical correlations between savings and the course of growth of the United States, Great Britain, Russia and elsewhere. Others are led toward their conclusions by reasoning that to give impetus to growth, many new undertakings must be carried forward at the same time. As lucidly expounded by Barbara Ward:

> To return to our economic rule of thumb—then when twelve to fifteen per cent of the national income is being directed to saving, to capital formation, the economy grows—it is important to grasp that the reason for such a percentage is not simply that it allows a country to keep ahead of its growth of population and to set more aside each year for saving; it is also that without a certain momentum of saving, development can remain patchy and the growth of each sector fails to assist the growth of all the rest, railways helping the ports, the ports helping the growing cities, the cities promoting markets for the farms, and factories providing external economies to each other. When the spiral of growth runs right through the economy it begins to be within sight of the break-through to sustained growth. But if capital formation remains below the level needed to create a sort of contagion of development, the result is what you see throughout the developing world where small segments of modernization co-exist with stagnant traditional areas and no full momentum of growth develops. So the problem in the first instance is how to achieve the accelerated rate of savings which will ensure a break-through to sustained growth.[7]

7. Barbara Ward, *The Rich and Poor Nations,* page 96.

Even more precise measurement of the imputed relationship between the part of annual national income invested and the rate of annual growth can be found in the professional literature. These estimates tend to cluster about the conclusion that to achieve an annual rate of growth of 2 to 3 per cent, at least 12 to 15 per cent of national productive effort will have to be devoted to the creation of capital goods; to achieve a growth rate of 5 per cent, about 20 per cent.

All such paradigms must be conditional on total national circumstances. The ratio between the portion of the net national product that is invested and the rate of economic growth is not the same for any two countries. Many elements will cause variations in different places and at different times. The presumption that there is a standard basis for reckoning how much capital will be needed to make possible a projected increase in per capita income over a period of years is dubious. Forecasts of how much growth will result from any designated volume of investment are fallible.

The magic that resides in capital is not constant nor invincible. It will work only when well used and favored by orderly and stable political and social circumstances. However, in their entrancement with the power attributed to capital—nations longing for easier and healthier lives are often inclined to disregard this demanding condition.

3 | Toward the Theory of Material Improvement: Continued

Qualifying conditions were also largely left out of account in attempts by eager sympathizers to figure out the total sums which would be required to speed the poorer countries on their way. As observed by Antonin Basch in his review of the usual formulation of the problem and the range of answers:

> Estimates are being worked out as to how much external aid the less developed countries will need until they can reach a level of capital formation sufficient for self-sustaining growth. The problem is often worded in this way: How much external aid is needed to increase the per capita income, say, by 2½ per cent annually assuming a 2 per cent yearly increase in population? The amount of aid is no longer linked to the foreign exchange gap but to the need of supplementing domestic resources. The annual amount of aid needed is often placed at $5–6 billion dollars. . . .[1]

Public opinion, especially in the United States, was impressed by such presumptively exact estimates of the amount of help re-

1. From *The Future of Foreign Lending for Development*, by Antonin Basch, published by the Center of Research of Economic Development, University of Michigan, Ann Arbor, Michigan, March, 1962, page 1.

quired to raise up the piteously poor parts of the world. The conclusions were simple and the designated sums within the range of what the wealthier countries could spare without great strain. Therefore advocates of aid to foreign countries for political, humane or commercial reasons found such estimates helpful in their pleadings and presentations. If the needed dollars (pounds, francs, marks) which could be turned into capital anywhere, were provided, the idea ran its course, then material progress everywhere, though slow, would be almost sure.

But experience soon upset this optimistic outlook. Encounters with the hard facts that ruled most poorer societies dimmed it. Theory and judgment, which had temporarily narrowed down to a simple formula, broadened again. They regained cognizance that what is achieved by capital in any poor country is in every way contingent upon climate, natural resources and geography, domestic and social customs and standards, religion and superstitions, political conditions and structure, literacy, attitude toward work and thrift, the distribution of property and income, and whether its disposition be peaceful or bellicose.

Theory re-emerged from its restrictive logical and statistical shells. In refreshed recognition that all these features of national life are determinants of economic affairs rather than—as is alleged in Marxian doctrines—merely an emanation of them, the newer formulations of the route to growth expanded to include them as causative facts. True, all are pliable under the influx of capital and changing techniques of production. But one and all affect both the possibility of accumulating capital and securing advanced techniques, and the results of their induction into the economy.

Theory adapted itself to the observed fact that to improve the condition of a country hitherto clearly unable to emerge from poverty, a transforming current must be sent coursing through *all* its arteries. The simpler formulas for promoting growth gave way to analyses which embrace and bring under inspection all facets of national society.

Concordantly, administrators of foreign aid also recognized the need to view each national situation as a whole in deciding what capital and technical assistance to provide. The change in attitude is expressed in the current inclination to insist that countries qualify themselves to make good use of the ingredients of growth rather than merely to trust to their inherent curative and nutrient powers. To this new emphasis on the importance of self-help we shall advert at greater length.

Both theory and practice thus have moved toward the conclusion that the treatment of each and every component of growth must be correlated. Or at least that main decisions involving large sums of loaned or given capital should be considered as elements in national plans or programs, and conform to them in size and phasing.[2]

The belief in the value—if not the necessity—of national planning or programing got its first great boost in the success of the Marshall Plan. Each of the participants developed and discussed with one another and with the American government a national prospectus for recovery. Their combined requirements for American aid in order to carry out the resultant programs were thereby roughly determined. Agreement was reached on the respective allocations; and on the scheduled activities which each would try to perform. The success of that joint plan left deep marks on professional theory as well as in American official thinking and practice. It was taken as confirmation of the value of a procedure whereby national goals were defined in advance and priorities established for both domestic capital and foreign aid. It was hailed

2. As lucid and convincing exposition of the reasons for this procedure as I have seen is Kenneth Galbraith's short essay, "The Need for a Comprehensive Plan and Program," and his article in *Foreign Affairs*, April 1961, "A Positive Approach to Foreign Aid."

as proof that growth could be successfully planned and guided without objectionable restraints and controls. For these and other reasons it was a persuasive precedent.

So persuasive that it was, perhaps, misleading. For it fostered the impression that the task of bringing about economic improvement everywhere else in the world would be easy, and almost assured. But how many other countries had capacities for quick recovery and growth equivalent to those of the members of the Marshall Plan? Their experience in the conduct of production, their high standards of general education, their fund of technical knowledge, their habit of saving, their capable financial institutions, their tradition of hard work and peaceful order under law were exceptional. Before long, the suppliers of aid were reminded of the importance of these qualifications by the failure of their programs in other countries.

It became clear that each planning procedure and prescription must fit the particular case, and differ from others in components, proportions and pace.[3]

In still another way current ideas about the route to economic growth diverge from earlier ones. No longer is the view unchallenged that competitive international trade should be the arbiter of the division of economic activity between countries. The drift of recent theoretical opinion is toward approval of the desire of most of the poorer countries to lessen their dependence on agricultural and other extractive activities. It admits the sensibleness of their wish to develop whatever local industries they can without

3. The extent and variety of national differences which must be considered are nowhere more fully and pertinently noted and explained than in the series of country Studies made by missions organized by the International Bank for Reconstruction and Development. Although they are primarily descriptive of existing resources, institutions and economic tendencies, most of them also draw attention to the important hindrances to economic growth, and suggest investment purposes and opportunities and make recommendations of policies to guide planning for national improvement.

Up to now, reports have been published on Ceylon, Colombia, Guatemala, Jamaica, Jordan, Libya, Malaya, Nigeria, Spain, Surinam, Syria, Thailand, Uganda, and Venezuela.

having to sacrifice too much of the advantages of cheap imports.

The change in the slant of theoretical judgment has been due primarily to the pressure of hard facts. Most countries that have relied primarily on production and exports of "primary" products have fared less well than have the more industrialized ones. Neither their incomes nor their earnings from exports have grown as much, and those of some have fallen.

So many of their people are unemployed that new industries may be developed and new constructions built without depriving farming and mining of labor needed to produce enough to satisfy both domestic and foreign demand.

Moreover, it is imperative that they should proceed to develop new branches of industry and enlarge established ones. For great numbers of their people who are leaving their villages and countryside to cluster in the cities and industrial centers are clamoring for jobs or relief.

These contemporary facts, in combination, have compelled an adaptation of theories of growth. These have become more lenient than their precursors to policies which are aimed at reducing dependence on primary industries, especially those which rely on foreign markets, and which encourage local industrial ventures even though they cannot compete with imports in the free market.

The migration of persons has been left out of the compass of these theories of economic growth that have been reviewed. Yet since it has often been, in the past, and could be again, the greatest catalyst of all, notes upon it may be interjected at this point.

The large migrations of the nineteenth and twentieth centuries were propelled by a variety of necessities and aspirations. Some were economic. New expanding countries beckoned to farmers and workers living in more crowded native lands in poverty and distress—ill-fed, ill-clothed, meanly housed. The more recently opened regions offered skilled and professionally trained persons better prospects of a career, and ambitious men a better chance to start a trade or business and become rich and independent. In short, they were allured by prospects of a better livelihood.

Other large migrations were escapes from oppression, constraints and danger. Among the most notable of such movements was the departure of liberals and radicals from Germany, Austria and France after the failure of the revolutions of the eighteen-forties, and the flight of the Jews from their ghettos and from pogroms in the time of the Czars in Russia and the monarchy in Rumania.

Except for limitations on entry of Oriental peoples into the Western world, there were few barriers to migration before the First World War. All that most persons needed were passage money, a health certificate and perhaps an employment contract. Most governments of the countries of origin were reconciled to the departure of natives who were a restless, unhappy and sometimes despised element in national life. By some authorities the exodus was encouraged to lessen the demand on food supplies, to get rid of persons living on charity, to reduce the numbers of children of poor families who had to be clothed, shod and schooled, and to reduce the number of adults among whom farmlands had to be divided or for whom work had to be found in workshops, stores, offices, building trades, or ships. Some countries such as Italy, Greece, Ireland, Norway, Hungary, Poland and Spain regarded the departure of their people with less regret since after they were settled in their new homes, they sent back remittances to their relatives and increased commerce with their homelands.

As in the past, most migrants must still make their own way, earn their own living by hard work, frugality and enterprise. Most of them are zealous to get ahead in their adopted land. The unskilled and uneducated may bring only stamina, the willingness to endure the fatigue of hard manual labor, heat and cold, the squalor of city slums or the loneliness of construction camps. Such were the sustaining qualities of the millions of migrants to the United States who broke stone and pounded gravel, mixed cement for roads, carried bricks and mortar for houses and tall buildings, laid pipes for sewers, cut timber and worked in saw-mills, mined coal and stoked furnaces, cleared and plowed land, strung fences, dug ditches and wells, cut and sewed clothes, trimmed hats in sweatshops. That so much of the United States was at that time undeveloped meant for the newcomers or their children opportunities for which they were willing to bear tribulations and hardships.

The more educated and those trained in some business or profession, inaugurated and stimulated new branches of production and services. They brought a useful knowledge of the outside world, higher standards of hygiene, and a strong desire for honest and responsible government.

Walk down any street in which business or professional offices, factories, stores and workshops are located in New York, Detroit, Cincinnati, Houston, Sydney, Toronto, Buenos Aires, Rio de Janeiro, São Paulo, Caracas, Mexico City, Kingston (Jamaica), Singapore, Haifa—and until recently, Algiers, Casablanca, Cairo—and note the names of the men and women who own or run the growing enterprises. Run through the roster of those who provide skilled services, who teach in the universities and laboratories. The names signify what the immigrants have done for their adopted lands.

Most of the countries that remain very poor in our time would similarly benefit from an influx of vigorous and ambitious foreigners. Virtually none of the applicants for American economic aid have enough trained people to make the best use of the capital they seek. The list of skills and professions for which newcomers should be sought is as long as the day: blueprint and instrument makers, electricians, drillers, loggers, machinists, mechanics of all kinds, telephone men, plumbers, surveyors for the preliminary work of road building and construction; for more technical tasks, engineers, chemists, physicists, biologists; and for business enterprise, men with a knowledge of manufacturing processes and products, and managers, accountants, bookkeepers and personnel directors; and for cultivation of the land, able farmers, animal breeders and irrigation specialists, handy men to take care of and repair tools and machines; for health and prolongation of life, doctors, pharmacists and nurses; for education, teachers; for the improvement of political and social institutions, judges, lawyers, historians and superior journalists; for the enhancement of daily life, as well as for self-understanding, novelists, dramatists, painters. I need not mention actors, singers and musicians for they will arise in every land and go wherever there is an audience. Nor must I mention economists or economic planners, for the poorest countries now court and welcome them. As to allowing bankers to enter and reside, each country must decide for itself. But foreign bankers may be content with a lower rate of interest than local ones, and may be more inclined to add to their fortunes by financing new ventures rather than by merely taking usurious advantage of beggary.

Many of the poorer countries now do not welcome immigrants —individuals of different racial origin or color. They do not want foreigners in their midst for fear of domination or competition, or because of dislike that is quickened by ignorance. But of those countries that have been ready to receive desirable immigrants only a few, those that are larger and more favorably endowed by nature, such as Brazil, are able to attract and keep them. Some fail to do so because they offer little economic attraction; others because their climate is harsh, or they lack educational and recreational opportunities; others because they are in chronic political and social turmoil.

From some of the poorest countries—former colonies who have gained independence—there has been a regrettable exodus, voluntary or enforced, of Europeans who had settled there in more (to them) pleasant and secure times. Many of these immigrants, some of whom had lived and worked in their adopted lands as long or longer than their present rulers—have departed from Tunis, Morocco, Algeria, Egypt, Tanganyika, Kenya, Ghana, the Congo, Rhodesia and other areas of subtropical Africa, Indonesia, Ceylon and Vietnam. Among them went many experienced and talented men and women vitally needed for progress.

They are even harder to replace than capital. The task of training an equivalent native group is difficult, slow, costly and uncertain. The admission and temporary employment of a hired corps of foreigners as consultants, advisers and instructors will not compensate for the loss. Nor will those large aggregations of foreign specialists which aid-giving governments, particularly those in the Communist bloc, send in to carry out large projects, such as the Aswan Dam in Egypt. The temporary residents may leave behind them a residue of knowledge and skill, diffused among many eager, able and ambitious natives. But a considerable lack will be felt for a long time, perhaps forever.

Whatever the cause of the exodus—whether it was voluntary or compelled—the countries abandoned by these productive elements have to start their climb out of poverty from a lower level and will find the climb more arduous. In their bitterness over the past, their high temper, their struggle for national independence and racial equality, they may have lost one valuable component of growth that history brought them. Both they and the wealthier countries to which they look for assistance will find it harder to compensate for the loss by providing other components.

We shall observe further, as we go along, how American practices in the use of foreign aid as an auxiliary to our diplomacy and strategy are being adopted to conform to the evolving ideas of how material improvement can be brought about.

4 | Toward the Affiliation Between Aid and Diplomacy

Some economists, political scientists and planners believe that if efforts in behalf of poorer countries are conducted with single-minded economic purpose, they will redound more to the peace and security of all than if they are at the beck and call of national diplomacy. But officials, diplomatic and military, and taxpayers of the contending contributors, answer in their thought if not in words, "Sorry, but circumstances compel us to use our power to give or refuse help in order to protect ourselves in a world that contains powerful rivals and enemies."

Many realities restrict and complicate the ways in which foreign policy can and should guide or even govern foreign aid. Our examination will gain meaning from a historical review of past attempts to concert the two. If it does no more, this may acquaint us with the involutions of the problems of decision.

Up to 1914 Western Europe was the main source of capital and technical knowledge for the less developed parts of the world. The fraction of their national incomes and savings which the people of Great Britain, France and Germany sent abroad during this pre-war era was greater than any similar outflow before or since.

"Gain" not "growth" was the password which opened the gates. Investors sought profit. To assist in the material betterment of the recipient countries was an approved and acclaimed result. But it was not a commonly acknowledged obligation of the suppliers of capital.

The governments of each of the three financial centers did not lose sight of the foreign ventures of their capitalists. They strove to assure that these served the national interest. The British government did so by circumspect silences or frowns; the French government by administrative control; the German government through institutional contact between the large banks and officialdom.

The British government had no formal regulatory system for foreign loans and enterprises. Laws were enacted which gave some inducement to purchase securities issued by the British colonies and dominions. But British investors were left free to decide for themselves where, how and when to lay out their capital. For such supervision as was thought necessary the British government relied upon the close personal associations within the small circle that ran international political and financial affairs. The responsible members of the government counted on the fact that those who wielded financial power usually had the same views about Britain's foreign policy and commercial interests as themselves. Thus the government ordinarily abstained from indicating an opinion about a contemplated transaction. If the financiers were in doubt they could inform themselves about official views by private inquiry. They were alert to information and hints passed out during luncheon at their clubs, or in country houses, and they took careful notice of signals that might be found in a speech in the House of Commons or at a political dinner, or in inspired articles in the press. With singular skill they kept themselves constantly well advised about the government's projected course in murky political areas. They strove constantly to do so, the better to gauge the future safety of their loans and investments.

The alignment within the same small orbit of those having official position and those having capital, the responsiveness to group opinion, the personal honesty and discretion of officialdom and of banking circles explain why the British government did not have to resort to any systematized arrangement to ensure that foreign operations of its financiers did not clash with British diplomacy or injure British interests.

British capital, thus ordinarily left to seek its own advantage, engaged largely in construction and operation of railways and other public utilities, and in development of new sources of foodstuffs and raw materials for which there was a ready market. It entered most readily into those countries in which European migrants were settling. It ventured most boldly and in greatest volume in countries under the British flag and in the United States —within the realm, that is, of reliable political friendship. British finance stayed out of countries toward which antipathy existed, being quick to detect possible breaks, no matter how muffled, in the rhythm of relations.

However, in the decade before the start of the First World War, as the rivalry between Great Britain and other great European powers for colonies, trade, strategic bases and control of natural resources became ominous, the British government intervened more actively in private lending and investment operations. In some countries in the Middle East, Asia and Africa where imperialisms were pacing each other, British diplomacy thrust its own capitalists forward and upheld their claims against rivals. They were warned not to engage in some transactions. They were encouraged to enter into others in order to court a friendship, nurse an alliance or solidify a sphere of influence. Contrary to the Marxian interpretation, in the association between finance and diplomacy the government more often than not took the initiative. Left to themselves the capitalists would have tended to allow pecuniary considerations to be supreme and, guided by their intuition, to keep clear of the stormy centers of international politics.

This intimate contact between British finance and diplomacy

seemed at the time to serve both well. Capitalists secured a superior income. The might and responsibilities of the Empire were upheld. Most of the countries in which British finance was engaged benefited notably from its activities and presence. Their production and trade were enlarged. Their material condition was improved. In the temperate Europeanized countries the whole economy was propelled forward by the influx of foreign funds and the initiatives of foreign financial and business groups; and all sections and classes of their people were in some way helped. But in many of the colonies, especially those in the tropics, the foreign-owned enterprises were separated from the rest of the local economy, which remained unaffected and as primitive, untaught and poor as before.

When war came in 1914, the external assets which had been acquired by its capitalists enabled Great Britain to pay for weapons, munitions, food and raw materials needed to sustain the struggle. The enlarged productivity of the countries and regions that had been nurtured by British capital and enterprise contributed heavily to victory.

Still this association between British finance and diplomacy (it is time to note its Scottish component, since Scots and Scottish acumen played so large a part in its direction) failed to achieve the ultimate political and economic objectives that must be sought through foreign aid. It brought neither the peace nor lasting plenty. For it did not eliminate the mistrusts and tensions between the European powers, or soothe their quarrels over territory, wealth and trade. Instead, the competition, here and there, between British capital and rival groups of other nations, each enlisting the support of its government, was one of the irritants that led to the tragic end.

During this same era the total annual national income and the per capita income of the French people were smaller than those of the British. Nevertheless, they saved a remarkably large fraction of it; by the turn of the century almost a billion dollars a year.

French agriculture, industry and commerce did not bid strenuously for so large a sum. Much of it was heaped up by peasants, storekeepers, merchants, owners of workshops and factories who did not use all of it in their own properties. Foreign borrowers offered high interest to savers, large commissions to French banks, and bribes to French newspapers and periodicals which helped them to float loans. Thus much of this saving sought the presumed liquidity and safety of bonds issued by foreign governments and companies.

French industry and commerce were torpid. French political destiny was being determined in a world that included rivals who might become enemies. French capital was one of the means by which French influence could be exerted and French alliances cemented. Moreover, the French government, and French commercial and banking interests were eager to enlarge the French colonial empire, and in that way to increase their trade and financial transactions. In the going competition for control of weak and primitive countries, French capital, in close association with French diplomacy, might procure for France a substantial part of the spoils. Most French people thought—as did most British and German—that the expansion of their empire was not only of advantage to their country but also civilizing and benign.

Swayed by these purposes and cravings, the government supervised the foreign engagements of French capital. By decree, financial groups intending to offer foreign securities for sale in France, and wishing to have them listed on its security exchanges, were required to secure official assent in advance. This legalized power to deny access to French capital markets was actively used. Decisions were slanted to suit official French political connections, antipathies and initiatives. Loans and investments were encouraged in countries aligned with French diplomacy. Most notably, under duress to sustain the alliance with Czarist Russia and induce it to make desired military dispositions, huge loans for the Russian government were arranged and bonds were sold by hundreds of branches of the great banks to thousands of small savers in every province and village of France. The imperial visage on Russian bonds was almost as well known—I cannot say domesticated—as the familiar figures on the advertising posters of the cafés chantant. Moreover, the Russian Foreign Office was consulted about proposed loans to other governments which might affect that country. France's Balkan allies were similarly favored. In contrast, loans to German and Austrian public authorities and investments in German and Austrian private enterprises were banned.

The official supervisors of French foreign financial activities often bargained for some concession, diplomatic or commercial, as the price for assent to the making of a loan. Their terms were often accepted by the more impecunious borrowers. By others they were compromised or refused. These practices created an air of *marchandage,* of bazaar haggling in the French capital market and tarnished French diplomacy.

Still out of the small black clasp purses and bank accounts of the French bourgeoisie, the Russian Czars drew the substance for their monumental plans, the Sultans of Turkey, Egypt, and Morocco were enabled to spend without keeping accounts, Italy was helped to strengthen its national unity, Portugal was enabled to live with dignity despite defaulted loans, and the small Balkan states aided in asserting their national existence. French capital also financed the installation of railways and bridges, the construction of ports, electric and gas works, and processing plants in Russia and down through the Balkans from Budapest to Istanbul and into Syria and Turkey, and flowed over into South American public utilities and mines. The shovels that had dug a canal from the Red Sea to the Mediterranean were set to dig another across the narrow strip of Panama—when yellow fever struck.

In the French colonies, plantations and vineyards were created, trading posts and towns laid out, and railways and tramways built near the capitals, and the channels of ports and rivers were cleared, and lighthouses erected—all due to the frugalities of the French peasants, the middle class, and to the lively and luxuriant imaginations of its bankers. But French capital and enterprise played only a small part in the sprouting of the economies of those great and fertile areas which were populated mainly by English-speaking peoples, or of countries within the realm of British influence.

How did this restless concert between French finance and diplomacy work out? In a word, woefully. The immense loans to the Czarist Government of Russia did uphold the alliance with that country. But because they sustained a decayed monarchy that suppressed movements to establish constitutional government and mismanaged military operations during the war, they fostered the situation in which Bolshevism was able to triumph. The denial of the chance to borrow—though justified by all ordinary tenets of diplomacy—accentuated the ominous hostility between France and Germany and Austria-Hungary.

War was not averted. France lost many of its gifted and courageous youth. The capitalists lost their foreign investments. Little survived of the economic growth or gain produced in the recipient countries by French capital. France was saved not by its subsidized European alliances but by the entry into the war of the United States. Victorious France regained border provinces and a shaky and temporary supremacy. It kept its Empire but that has subsequently disintegrated.

Germany appears in history as a poor country. Voltaire prophesied that it was condemned to eternal poverty. But by the start of the twentieth century its concentrated banking system found the means not only to finance the great impulsion of trade and industry within Germany but also to accommodate some foreign borrowers and implant German enterprise abroad. Since the volume of German capital was not enough to meet all domestic needs and respond to all foreign opportunities, it was carefully budgeted.

The outward flow, like that of British capital, was determined mainly by financial reckoning and the desire for trade and foreign sources of food and raw materials. While ministering to these purposes, it was made also to serve German diplomacy and the desire for colonies and spheres of influence.

The large banks that dominated German finance consulted the German Foreign Office about foreign loans to which a political interest might attach or to which serious objection might be taken. As their interests increased in regions where the safety of the investment depended upon the support of the German government, they took more pains to make their decisions conform to official wishes. The government discouraged the banks from entering into transactions which might transgress German diplomacy. For example, negotiations for loans to the governments of Russia, Serbia and Bulgaria were curbed and German stock exchanges were closed to new listings of Russian government securities. The flow of German capital into Italy, at one time large, was slacked off as relations with that country grew unreliable.

More irritant were the active steps taken by the government to serve its political purposes or to uphold German interest in disputed vulnerable areas. In certain of these the German government vied with the British or French or Russian or with all of them—as the case was—to secure for German capital the chance to share in a loan, or to build a railway or finance an industry. Now and again it overruled the hesitation of banks or security buyers to accept the risk of loss. For example, it took the lead in arranging for the penetration of German capital into the Ottoman Empire, Morocco, China and into some parts of Africa that might be annexed by a rival.

As the struggle over the balance of power became fiercer, German finance revealed the same traits as German foreign policy; pushfulness and a rasping rudeness, due in part to a chafing sense of the injustice of history which had given rivals earlier and easier opportunities.

The triumphs in the contest for trade, control of natural resources and for colonies did not satisfy German ambitions. But they alarmed the other great powers who feared armed German might, discipline, and hardness. The extrusion of German capital and industry, made bold by the German government, was one of the causes of friction that led to war. With defeat, the creative contributions of German foreign loans and investments to the growth of other countries were almost wholly destroyed or depreciated.

The competitive efforts of the greater European powers before the First World War to enlist their capital in the service of their diplomacy leave the historian with a cautionary tale ending in grim truisms. Competitive investment in poor and weak countries conjoined with political and trade deals can turn out to be lethal for all. Financial power may for a while effectively aid national diplomacy, bringing victory in some contested areas or situations. But if the rivals are nearly equal in military strength, the possession of means to lend to others or invest abroad will not be of decisive avail. It may prolong the time granted to statesmen to convert enmity into comity. But if this is not done, most or all of the creative constructions of foreign aid will be reduced to ashes. The vision of parallel material improvement and social progress will turn out to have been an illusion.

Before and during the First World War, the American government, by force of arms, imposed control over the finances of the Dominican Republic, Haiti, Nicaragua and Honduras. It wanted to enable American and European holders of bonds that had been sold by these governments to collect interest and it tried to protect the lives and properties of Americans and Europeans who were engaged in business in these countries. At the time it was believed that unless the United States took over in this way some aggrieved European power might do so, justifying its action by the defaults or misconduct of these countries. They had, it was concluded, to be taught, if necessary by compulsion, to be financially responsible and to end the perpetual political disturbances that were dooming them to poverty.

American intervention did bring to some of the small Caribbean and Central American countries a measure of financial and political order, if not of popular freedom. However, their peoples—especially the younger politicians—became restless under American presence and control. They strained against the severe restraints of American financial advisers, and were offended by the harsh commands of the American military men in their midst. They were resentful of the privileged position of American-owned enterprises, and critical of the high interest and commissions collected on some American loans. The name "dollar diplomacy" was pinned on our handling of the troubled financial-political situations in the small countries of the region.

After the First World War, American capital roamed further and in much greater amounts. In their sprouting self-assurance Americans were disposed to take on the next jobs; to clean up the rubble of the war and put the world, especially Europe, on its feet again. Most were unwilling, as the outcome of the national debate about joining the League of Nations showed, to share in the anxieties and risks of keeping peace in the world. But American energy, shrewdness, honesty, skill—and above all else, American dollars—were disponible.

Great Britain had been compelled to sell most of its foreign securities. It was in debt to foreigners for purchases made during the war, and had barely enough foreign means to begin to repair and revive its depleted and dislocated economy. Although the thrifty French were better able to take care of themselves, they had nothing to lend others. Germany was in financial disorder and economic distress although it had suffered little physical destruction. Switzerland, Holland and Sweden had grown richer, but their resources were relatively small and their investment habits prudent. The only country with ample capital to which others could turn was the United States.

Americans were ready to risk their capital to get the high promised returns. American investment and banking houses sensed the temper and grasped the chance. Except for a few of the more far-

sighted, they arranged foreign loans and financed foreign investments with a careless swagger, and basked in the great and quick
commissions and profits.

The authorities tended to favor this exuberant response to foreign requests for loans. They believed that, except for emergency
relief, it would be inadvisable for the American government itself
to make loans or grants. As tersely stated by Secretary of State
Charles Evans Hughes, in August 1923: "It is not the policy of our
government to make loans to other governments, and the needed
capital if it is to be supplied at all, must be furnished by private
organizations. . . ."

The chief officials of all three administrations in office during
the twenties—those of Harding, Coolidge, and Hoover—were disposed to allow American financial interests and foreign seekers of
capital freedom to arrange their own deals. They thought it best
that ordinarily the dollar should conduct its own diplomacy, select
its own assignments, and make its own terms. Yet, like their European predecessors, they wished to guard against the chance that a
projected financial operation might harm American public interest
or foreign policy. The capital lent might be used for bad or wasteful purposes. Or it might enable a foreign government to ignore
our wishes or their conceived obligations to the United States.
Moreover, those in authority were unwilling to renounce entirely
the chance of using their power to push or prevent a loan as an aid
in diplomatic or trade negotiations.

The chief American investment houses and banks were asked to
inform the State Department in advance of all contemplated foreign transactions and await its judgment before acting. Func-
tionaries in the State and Commerce Departments—in touch with
the Treasury—watched, sometimes questioned, and now and again
let it be known that they liked or disliked a proposed deal. In this
confidential consultation the American government stayed behind
a screen from whence were wafted like spirit messages its opinions about proposed foreign loans and investments.

The most consequential use of this official power was to compel the former allies of the United States to sign agreements to repay the loans which the American government had made to them during the war. This demand had strong domestic political appeal (Coolidge: "They hired the money, didn't they?"). At the behest of the Treasury, American private financial markets were closed to them until they promised to repay. This policy had the most regrettable international effects of any American official action except the refusal to join the League of Nations. It was a continuing cause of bad feeling between the United States and its former allies in the war and of alienation from them. The call for repayment made them more obdurate in their demands for reparations from Germany, and that prolonged economic and monetary instability in Europe.

While former Allied governments were debarred from American financial markets, our banks and investment houses were beckoned to arrange loans to the German government in connection with negotiated reductions in the reparation payments which it was required to make. These American loans helped to start Germany on the road to economic recovery. The American bankers, the American people, and the American government were impressed both by the seemingly chastened spirit of the Germans and the capable way in which they were restoring their civilian industrial life. Thus, it came about that during the decade after the end of the First World War American capitalists loaned to and invested more in Germany—to public authorities, industries and banks—than in any other country. In the congeries of states into which the former Austrian-Hungarian Empire had been divided, American capital also became heavily engaged. Long-term credits to the financial institutions of those countries were supplemented by short-term, and presumably liquid, banking credits, so large in volume that when the crash began in 1929, many American banks had risked therein sums greater than their total capital. Italy was similarly well treated in consonance with the idea that Mussolini was restoring its vitality and credit worthiness. These transactions were at the time thought to be not only sound, but a contribution toward the prosperity and stability of all of Europe. It may be that by favoring this infusion of American capital into Europe many Americans eased their minds or consciences about the refusal to join the League of Nations and to accept a share in collective responsibility for maintaining peace.

Next in amount to American loans to European borrowers during this splurging decade of the nineteen-twenties was the investment of American industries in subsidiary plants in Canada and the British Dominions.

Hardly less were the sums loaned to Latin American governments. The terms accepted by those perpetual debtors were seductive. At the time, the American government smiled upon this overflow of largesse to Latin America. However, now and again it did repress a proposed transaction. It cautioned banks to abstain from lending to governments that did not have popular support. It objected to the provision of more funds to those who were mismanaging their finances and who were willing to go more deeply into debt in order to continue on their wanton way. It prevented loans for the enlargement of military organizations.

When turned down for these reasons, eager pursuers of loans sometimes managed to get around American official obstruction. They borrowed for other avowed approved purposes and then used their own funds to finance discredited ones. But the ban was, in general, effective against governments which the United States was refusing to recognize either because they were mistreating American interests or because they were deemed oppressive and corrupt.

In one area American diplomacy openly teamed up with American enterprise-capital. They concerted their determined effort to procure for American interests a fair part of the opportunity to develop the vast oil resources of the Middle East which the British and French oil companies and governments were trying to monopolize. The American government acted on the belief that it was essential to American security that American companies have participation substantially in ownership of the oil of that region. Its protests were indignant, since even before American entry into the war the United States had responded to desperate appeals from Great Britain and France for greater shipments of oil from our domestic reserves that had to be transported to them over submarine-haunted oceans.

For a time, the American government restrained bankers from arranging loans to Japan. It was disturbed by the creeping Japanese domination over Manchuria, and did not want to displease China by having Americans provide the resources to enable Japan to go further. However, during the late twenties, when the Japanese government seemed to be pursuing a moderate and peaceful policy, and after Japan had entered into treaties designed to maintain order in the Pacific and protect the integrity of China, the American government relaxed its opposition. Thereby it hoped to strengthen the influence of the more peacefully inclined elements within Japan.

To all publicly-issued loans for the government of the Soviet Union the American government stood firmly opposed. The reasons were summarized by Secretary of State Hughes in 1923 shortly after the boundaries of the Soviet Union were settled and its government was trying to borrow wherever it could: "Not only would it be a mistaken policy to give encouragement to repudiation and confiscation, but it is also important to remember that there should be no encouragement to the effort of those Soviet authorities to visit upon other people the disasters which have overwhelmed the Russian people." This view was bluntly reiterated whenever the question arose, as in February 1928 when the State Department informed the press that it did not ". . . view with favor financial arrangements designed to facilitate in any way the sale of Soviet bonds in the United States." In any case there would not have been much of a market in the United States for Soviet securities. But official objection was not carried to the point of preventing American banks from giving short-term credits to Russian state organizations to finance American exports such as cotton, nor to void those contracts whereby large American corporations sold their products to the Russian government trusts on credit.

The outcome of these attempts during the twenties to keep the foreign activities of American capital in conformity with foreign policy and ideals is clear. The war-damaged and socially-disturbed countries of Western Europe were assisted in their crawl back toward economic health, thereby checking the intrusion of Communism. Some of the discords left by the war and the peace treaties were temporarily soothed. Tensions between the United States and much of Latin America were eased, and promising new economic developments went forward in the lands to the south of us.

But this progress toward political tranquility and material improvement came to an end as economic depression and financial panic spread and worsened, and as Europe fell back again into political turmoil. Central European financial institutions, to which American banks had so open-handedly loaned their own liquid funds, collapsed. Their governments went bankrupt. Their industries were unable to pay either debts or dividends. Virtually all Latin American governments defaulted on their bonds.

As an agent of diplomacy, or as sound financial ventures, these first large external operations of American capital were quickly adjudged to have been a foolish mistake. A general sigh of resolve was heard through the United States: never again, the American people vowed, would they lend or invest their money in foreign lands. During the years that followed, they strove to dissociate their country from the rest of the world.

The experience evoked one of Franklin D. Roosevelt's campaign charges. On August 20, 1932, he said that if he were elected he promised that,

> . . . it will no longer be possible for international bankers or others to sell foreign securities to the investing public of America on the implied understanding that these securities have been passed on or approved by the State Department or any other agency of the Federal Government.

There never was any such misunderstanding. The trouble lay much deeper: misjudgment of what dollars could do unless linked with a wise and courageous diplomacy and a forward-looking economic policy. The sense of duty to assist in the material improvement of other countries perished in the depths of American troubles and losses.

This mood had regrettable consequences. During the subsequent crucial decade it caused the American government and people to make the opposite blunder. They renounced—it might also be said denounced—the idea of using American capital and productive power to assist diplomacy and influence the course of events in the outside world. American capital, hard hit and scared, ceased to invest abroad.

The American government did not step in to supply the financial aid which private investors no longer forwarded. It gave little economic help to China, even after Japan grasped Manchuria in defiance of us and the League of Nations. It did almost nothing to sustain and strengthen the countries menaced by the rise of National Socialism in Germany. It stood by as Mussolini—with cruelty and deceit—acquired a stucco empire along the shores of the Eastern Mediterranean and Africa, shook the League of Nations, and in combination with Hitler, defeated democracy in Spain.

The great and sparable American economic and financial resources could have been made to count greatly during these years. As soon as the nature and intentions of the Axis were evidenced, American government and finance should have stepped forward and offered its opponents means to enlarge their industrial capacity and military forces. Had the United States, during the thirties, lent or given Great Britain, France, China and their associates sums equal to those provided later on under the Marshall Plan, this might have made the difference between peace and war. But such initiative was debarred by the dominant nature of American foreign policies during these years. Having failed in its attempts to organize peace by treaty law, the United States strove to be neutral, isolated, unoffending. The American people shirked and evaded the impending necessity to increase their armed forces mightily and quickly.

With our performance during this period in mind, I wrote in 1950 when the American government was starting on its new great programs of foreign aid—"At best it is hard to foresee the ultimate political results of providing capital [and technical and other assistance] to many of the foreign nations which seek it. Regimes come and go. Alliances form, break, and re-form. Loyalties shift. The relative strength of nations changes over a period of time. Thus, even when a nation's foreign policy is well reckoned and clear, the task of directing its foreign aid over a span, say, of three decades, is more or less like pinning the tail on the donkey blindfolded. When the foreign policy is neither adequate nor clear, it is not possible to know even where the donkey is. That was the case in the two decades between the wars." [1]

The United States has, I believe, learned much since then. But the truth of this observation has still to be tested in our own trying times.

1.   *The Diplomacy of the Dollar,* page 65.

5 | Toward the Affiliation Between Aid and Diplomacy: Continued

During and after the Second World War the wheel of experience and decision revolved full turn. Ever since, the American government has, as an element of its foreign policy, made intense efforts to assist other countries.

The United States was generous in the relief donated to victims of the Second World War. The American government brought into existence the United Nations Relief and Rehabilitation Administration (UNRRA), providing about three quarters of its funds. This organization distributed drugs, clothing, raw materials, seeds and farm implements to the people of forty countries that had suffered from Axis attacks. The deed brought hope and health to millions of those whom the war had left sick, alone, poor, adrift and homeless. But some of the countries and peoples in central and southeastern Europe most helped by UNRRA are now members of the Communist bloc and supporters of the Warsaw Pact. The occurrence illustrates how humane actions may be tripped up by the malicious turns of international politics.

During the same interim period President Truman, poorly advised, ended Lend-Lease aid. His administration was also hard-fisted in the negotiations of loans which the British government contracted to carry its people through the austere years that followed the exhausting war and the termination of Lend-Lease. The sum lent was too little; the promises exacted in regard to Britain's monetary policies proved to be too restrictive.

While wary lest their former allies take advantage of them, the American people resigned themselves to the need to give large grants-in-aid to former enemies—Germany, Japan and Italy—as well as to other areas in which American troops were stationed. American military and civilian representatives in the occupied countries were alarmed about what might happen if their people were not fed, clothed, housed and given hope.

American private investors and industries remained prudent stay-at-homes. They strayed only into such safe havens as Canada and Australia. Elsewhere their only important ventures were to develop a natural resource, such as oil, copper, bauxite, gold and diamonds, for which there was an assured market in the United States.

In short, during these first post-war years (1945–1947) the use of power to assist other peoples was sluggish. It was barely enough to enable the free countries of western and southern Europe, the Philippines and Japan to make a slow start toward restoration of their civilian economies and financial systems. Thereby their grave internal political troubles were slightly eased. None succumbed to the lure or agitations of Communism. But the danger that one or another might do so remained imminent.

For the Soviet Union had turned into an antagonist. Communist parties in France, Italy, Belgium and elsewhere were growing more solid, stronger, and more daring. A civil war in Greece was dragging on, and the British government was growing weary of the burden of sustaining resistance against the strong Communist forces in that country. Conditions in Turkey were so disturbed that it seemed possible that the torso of the former immense Ottoman Empire might disintegrate and that the Soviet Union might secure control of part of Turkish territory and the Dardanelles Straits. In that event, the Communists might have within their grasp the whole Mediterranean area.

In March, 1947, an aroused President (Truman) advised Congress that the United States should and must "support free people who are resisting attempted subjugation by armed minorities or by outside pressure . . . and . . . assist free peoples to work out their own destinies in their own way." Not only military support was needed, he explained, but economic and financial help. Congress responded to the embattled call. In order to prove that freedom was not synonymous with poverty, the American government agreed to give the Greek and Turkish governments what they needed.

From then on the American government began systematically to use our productive power to combat the over-reaching Communist activity and menace. Communist seizure of control in Czechoslovakia early in 1948 quickened fears that this might also happen in Austria, Italy, France and elsewhere in Western Europe since their economic revival was still lagging and popular discontent rising. In swift interim action emergency relief was given to Italy, Trieste and Austria. The European Recovery Program (the Marshall Plan) to brace up sixteen faltering countries in Europe was launched before the year was out. Secretary of State Marshall urged that our action should be substantial and sustained enough to be a cure rather than a palliative. The annual installments were approved by Congress as providing "aid to end aid." At the end of its four-year span most of the recipients were well on their way to prosperity and could dispense with American aid for ordinary economic undertakings.

While the United States was infusing the economies of its companions with new vigor, it joined with them in a mutual defense pact (NATO). Because its allies then could not at that time contribute much to joint defense without straining their fiscal ability and their balance of payments, the American government provided the supplementary means needed to enable them to do what was necessary.

While the Marshall Plan operations were under way, the attention of America was commanded by other parts of the world—the Middle East, the Far East, Latin America and Africa. These regions were in President Truman's mind when in his Inaugural Address in January 1949 he stated:

> We must embark on a bold new program for making the benefits of our scientific advances and industrial progress available for the improvement and growth of undeveloped areas.
> More than half of the peoples of the world are living in conditions approaching misery. Their food is inadequate. They are victims of disease. Their economic life is primitive and stagnant. Their poverty is a handicap, a threat both to them and to more prosperous areas. . . .
> I believe that we should make available to peace-loving peoples the benefit of our store of technical knowledge in order to help them realize their aspirations for a better life. And, in cooperation with other nations, we should foster capital investment in areas needing development.
> Our aim should be to help the free peoples of the world through their own efforts, to produce more food, more clothing, more materials for housing and more mechanical power to lighten their burdens.

In the law (Act for International Development) which gave effect to this proposal, the American government for the first time expressed a continuing intention to help all poor people to better themselves. A policy statement, which has remained standard in American official thinking and purpose ever since, was written in its preamble:

> It is declared to be the policy of the United States to aid the efforts of the peoples of economically undeveloped areas to develop their resources and improve their living and working conditions by encouraging the exchange of technical knowledge and skill and the flow of investment capital to countries which pro-

vide conditions under which such technical assistance and capital can effectively and constructively contribute to raising standards of living, creating new sources of wealth, increasing productivity, and expanding purchasing power.

This endeavor that reached beyond diplomacy was soon linked closely with diplomacy. The years 1949 and 1950 were traumatic. The Soviet Union exploded its first atomic weapon. Most Americans derived little reassurance from President Truman's avowal, in his announcement of the event, that "Ever since atomic energy was first released by man, the eventual development of this new force by other nations was to be expected. This probability has always been taken into account by us." They realized that their supremacy of power had come to an end, and they foresaw that as the years went by the Soviet Union would affront and assail the West more boldly. While Americans were adjusting to that nascent reality, China, on whose cooperation the United States had counted for security in the Pacific, fell before the triumphant Communists. Most percussive of all, in 1950, from the north, Korean Communists, trained and armed by the Soviet Union, swooped down upon South Korea. The American positions in Japan and the Philippines were threatened; the value of our main naval and air base in Okinawa depreciated.

These events left our complacency in shreds. The American people responded to the need to demonstrate their vitality and ability to defend the still undominated parts of the world and lead them onward toward growth. American foreign policy was refashioned. American diplomacy became blunter. After astoundingly quick and strong actions to save South Korea and prevent the Chinese Communists from taking Taiwan (Formosa), the United States began in earnest to become a nation under arms.

The program of foreign aid and support was primed to serve American diplomacy and military plans better. American capital, technical knowledge and constructive energy were set hard at work in foreign lands. Fewer Americans continued to harbor the illusion that our dollars (to use this colloquial description for our productive powers) could substitute for either military strength or fateful international engagements. But they were more disposed to use our dollars in the cause of security and freedom—for as much as they were worth.

Since the successive measures taken between now and then to assist in the material improvement of other countries—especially the poorer ones—have been so fully described by others, and since they are still so alive in current memory and literature, here I shall only remind of the more important acts and new departures.[1]

An aroused and angered Congress in 1950–51 approved large special allocations for South Korea and Taiwan to enable those menaced countries to support large military forces and to enable them to make work for their people on land and in new industries. The Philippine government was also helped to straighten out its finances and deal with conditions in the poorest areas of its islands. By stages, the shift of emphasis and expenditure to other poor and distant parts of the Orient, the Middle East and Africa was confirmed. The programs that evolved became more numerous and varied. Under the tension of international politics they were warped into complicated combinations of loans and grants to support foreign military forces and sustain the weakened economies of more than a score of countries in these regions. In all of them the Communists were pushing and plotting against the Western capitalist countries.

Toward the Latin American countries till almost the end of the fifties, the American government was parsimonious. Mistakenly it was thought that they could procure adequate means of development from private lenders and investors and that they should make a greater effort to do so. American diplomacy was inattentive, slow to appreciate that the countries to the south felt neg-

1.   Of all the many historical, statistical and analytical records none is more comprehensive or instructive than a recent one, *U.S. Private and Government Investment Abroad,* edited by Professor Raymond F. Mikesell, University of Oregon Books, 1962.

lected because the United States was not afraid that they might cause trouble. The distressing social conditions prevailing in many of them were ignored—until signs of discontent and impending revolutions shocked us into action.

Belatedly the American government summoned up its economic power to hold its position in this hemisphere. A series of special measures almost prodigal as compared with the past, were enacted. At the Conference of the Organization of American States in Bogotá in September, 1960, the American government promised to contribute a half billion dollars to establish an Inter-American Fund for Social Development to be used for the improvement of the land and rural living conditions, housing for the very poor, water supply and sanitation, education and technical training, and for the mobilization of the domestic resources of all members. An Inter-American Bank was created. At the Conference at Punta del Este we brought about, in 1961, the formation of the Alliance for Progress to which the American government is pledged to make large annual contributions.

In all, the American government has each year since 1950 provided sums approximating three billion dollars to sustain the struggling poor countries of the world and to stimulate their economic advancement and social betterment.

Each step in the profusion of its assistance among an ever increasing number of claimants was regarded at the time as necessary and expedient. Each of the many adaptations in the government structure that administered the aid program was hopefully hailed as a correction of the mistakes and deficiencies of the past. Yet during the last two years confidence in the efficacy of what has been done and is being done has waned. The popular belief, once so sure and upcast in the regenerative power of foreign aid in its diplomatic value, has drooped. As the committee of which General Lucius Clay was chairman reported—with a dash of relish—to the President in March, 1963, "There has been a feeling that we are trying to do too much for too many too soon, that we are over-extended in resources and under-compensated in results, and that no end of foreign aid is either in sight or in mind." [2]

The reasons why will become plain I believe after examining, as we shall in the following chapters, the tasks assumed by the government, the hindrances and dilemmas met. But before doing so it would be well to take note of the course of American *private* foreign investment. For that also figures largely in present consideration of how the aid programs of the American government should be constituted and directed.

American private foreign investment revived. It grew rapidly and zestfully as Europe began to thrive, and American commercial and financial connections spread.

The lesser part has been of the kind called "portfolio" investment—the purchase of bonds issued by foreign companies, foreign governments and international financial agencies (such as the International Bank for Reconstruction and Development), and of the stocks of foreign companies. The nominal value of the foreign securities of these types now owned by Americans may now be more than ten billions of dollars; some are payable in dollars, others in foreign currencies.

Moreover, during the last few years, American purchases of foreign bonds and stocks has tended to rise rapidly because interest rates in this country on long-term loans were comparatively low and the credit standing of borrowers had improved. Until almost yesterday this was regarded with equanimity, as pridefully proving that this country was the world's great international financial center. But continued large losses of gold, creating alarm about the stability of the dollar, has led to a reappraisal of the

2. Report to the President of the United States from the Committee to Strengthen the Security of the Free World—on the *Scope and Distribution of United States Military and Economic Assistance Programs*—Department of State—March 20, 1963. This will be cited hereinafter as the Clay Committee Report.

advisability of such exports of American capital—almost all to prosperous countries not seriously short of capital. Thus in July 1963, in an attempt to stem these purchases, President Kennedy requested Congress to impose an "interest equalization" tax on foreign bonds and stocks that might in the future be bought by Americans from foreigners. Since the poor countries have few securities that tempt American investors they would not be substantially affected. Responsive to Canadian protests, the President decided to ask Congress for discretional authority to "permit tax-free purchases of new issues needed to maintain the unimpeded flow of trade and payments" between the United States and any designated country. It is probable that the legislation enacted will contain other exceptions.

Of more dynamic importance has been the radiation of American industry. More than three thousand American industrial and commercial companies have acquired or set up since the end of the war over ten thousand new overseas branches, subdivisions and owned affiliates in all parts of the world. The imputed present value of these private "direct" investments is well over forty-one billion dollars. It has been growing at a rate of about four billion dollars per year. More than half of this increment has come from the reinvestment of local earnings and of reserves set aside to take care of depreciation.

As in the earlier era of American industrial expansion abroad, most of this direct private investment has been made in countries where the task of establishing and operating a business was neither too novel nor too trying; where the prospective market and purchasing power for the product was ample, and the local attitude friendly. More than a third of the investment went into Canada and other British Dominions, approximately a fifth into Western Europe, and a rapidly growing portion of the rest into Latin America. Little more than a tenth of the total went into the Middle East, Africa and Asia. By far the greater part of the recent additional private investment in these poorer and less developed regions has been, as in earlier periods, in the extractive or plantation industries: oil above all else, bauxite, iron ore, manganese, copper, rubber, sugar and bananas; only a small portion has gone up to now into manufacturing and commerce.

However, the enterprises financed by American capital are becoming more varied in character and showing more interest in countries hitherto dismissed as too poor or too risky. This is occurring despite the animus against private foreign capital that extends in some of the countries which most need what our intrusive but creative technology can do for them; and despite latent popular dislike or envy of those advantaged American groups that form in the wake of foreign American business—profit seeking and living more or less apart from the local community.

The American managers of business enterprises in foreign countries have been learning to please local authorities and to adapt to local pride and sentiments. They have improved their own business habits. They are reinvesting much of their profits, inviting local partnership, showing more perception in selection of their personnel, and demonstrating their willingness to train and educate native workers and technicians. As I write, there is a resurgence of the view that foreign countries should be taught more incisively that if they want to progress economically, they should court private capital, domestic and foreign, rather than appeal to foreign governments; a reversion toward the conviction of the nineteen-twenties.

As great as American public aid and the surge of American private foreign investments have been, the rate at which other countries have been increasing their contributions to the poor and undeveloped parts of the world has been growing even faster. This outflow of aid is one of the resilient features of the economic advance of both our former allies and of our former enemies—in the Second World War. The annual sum of public loans made by their governments and private investments made by their capitalists are becoming almost as great in amount as ours. But American grants and gifts are still unmatched.[3]

This foreign activity is being hailed by the American government. Any lingering concern for national prestige or rivalry for national influence has given way to a wish to see the total amount of aid given needy countries enlarged and the call upon the United States reduced.

That all, including the United States, can do more is beyond question. That all will have to do more if truly determined to try hard to rid the world of acute poverty is a conclusion that will impose itself on anyone who faces up to the dimensions and difficulties of the task.

3. The Clay Committee estimated that the bilateral economic assistance extended by the countries of Western Europe, Japan and Canada to other countries in 1963 will be about 2.5 billions of dollars.

In 1962 the French government dispensed about 900 million dollars for all purposes—more than half for technical assistance and economic equipment, the rest to finance budget deficits of local governments, education, public health, governmental tasks and public utilities. But almost all of this went into the franc area, both the public assistance and private investment, former French colonies or overseas dependencies, departments and territories. The recipient that got most was Algeria. French private foreign investment was about 450 millions. By far the largest private investment has been in the oil fields of the Sahara region.

In the same year the British government provided about 360 million dollars to members of the Commonwealth and dependent territories, and over 50 millions to foreign countries—as grants, technical assistance and loans. However, the British government and public institutions are probably educating, training and supplying more teachers, nurses and administrators from and for the poorer countries—particularly members of the Commonwealth—than any other Western country. British direct private investment in 1962 —excluding oil and insurance in foreign branches, subsidiaries and associates— was over 600 million dollars, largely re-investment of earnings.

Part two |

PRESENT ACTUALITIES

6 | Our Activating Political Aims

American officials have tried hard to convince Congress and the country that the job of helping other people to better themselves should be assumed as a chance to use our creative capability rather than an irksome necessity. So President Truman said in effect, as has been noted, in presenting his famous Point IV Program. So avowed Congress a decade ago in approving the early Acts for International Development. So again did President Kennedy in the message on foreign aid he sent to Congress in March 1961:

> There exists, in the 1960's, an historic opportunity for a major economic assistance effort by the free industrialized nations to move more than half the people of the less-developed nations into self-sustained growth, while the rest move substantially closer to the day when they, too, will no longer have to depend on outside assistance.[1]

1. None of the official American presentations in the cause of foreign aid—not even President Truman's Point IV message—matched in eloquent carefree fervor the appeal made and commitment given by de Gaulle, when on October 8, 1958, at Constantine he was appealing to Algerians to remain loyal to France. ". . . What must be achieved is the basic transformation of this country, so brave, so alive, but also so full of difficulties and suffering. This

While pleased by the vision of the constructive and humane possibilities, most Americans have supported our foreign aid activities in the belief that they preserve national security and freedoms under law.

Even if the Western world had not been menaced by international Communism, economic aid given by the American government to other countries would have been expanded much during the past decade and a half. Several trends of American thought, feeling and circumstance would have brought this about: a conscience more sensitive about the wretched plight of many other peoples; the wish to uphold the United Nations; an inclination to help other countries to achieve or maintain democratic political order and freedom; and the longing of our farmers, manufacturers and traders for foreign markets. But none of these has been as strong a stimulant to quick and bold action as the struggle against Communism. That has been the most energizing cause of American liberality, and often the incisive reason in the determination of what countries were helped by us most, and most urgently.

In the annual presentations made to committees of Congress and other audiences by platoons of officials headed by the President and the Secretary of State, the menace of Communism has been to the fore. A brief extract from an address made by President Kennedy (in the interval since sending the foreign aid message from which I have just quoted he had met with Khrushchev in Vienna) will serve to represent the many plans which played upon this anxiety.

> . . . the so-called wars of liberation Mr. Khrushchev has described cannot be stopped by a B-38 Squadron. They cannot be

means that it is necessary for the living conditions of each man and woman to improve from day to day. This means that the resources of the earth and the abilities of the people must be brought to light and developed. This means that children must be taught. This means that all Algeria must have her share in what modern civilization can and must bring to men in terms of well-being and dignity. But the loftiest plans call for practical measures."

deterred—these internal movements—by military guarantees. They cannot for the most part be resisted by American intervention in the absence of outside Communist troop intervention.

I therefore urge those who want to do something for the United States, for this cause, to channel their energies behind the new foreign-aid program to help prevent the social injustice and economic chaos upon which subversion and revolt feed; to encourage reform and development, to stabilize new nations and encourage weak governments, train and equip the local forces upon whom the chief burden of resisting local Communist subversion rests.[2]

Another excerpt from this same 1961 address may also be recalled to point up the contrast to President Kennedy's acquiescence two years later in recommendations of the Clay Committee —appointed by him—that the foreign aid program be much reduced and slowed down.

Now I know there are those who are tired of carrying what they regard as a burden, and it is a burden. But if they say that, then they mean they are tired of the struggle. And the struggle is reaching the climax in the sixties. And as I am not tired of the struggle and you're not tired of the struggle, and this country isn't tired of struggling, we should be willing to pay and bear our burdens in this regard for a longer period of time. And if we are tired of that then we should recognize the implication of that fatigue.

But when Congress revealed its intent to cut the sums allocated for aid far more drastically than seemed wise, his protests showed that his belief in the wisdom of continuing the effort to rout poverty—both as a duty and as a shield against Communism—had not really wavered. Sometimes in the course of his effort to overcome resistance to his requests, he emphasized one justifying purpose, sometimes the other, and usually he blended the two.

Thus in the comment which he made at his press conference on November 14, 1963, on the action of the Senate, President Ken-

2. Talk to National Conference on International Economic and Social Development. *The New York Times,* June 17, 1961.

nedy called the aid program ". . . essential to the conduct of our foreign policy" and said that if Congress denied him the required means of conducting that policy "they should recognize that they're severely limiting my ability to protect the National interest." And when asked if he was preparing to cope with a negative action by Congress, he answered, "No. I can't believe the Congress is going to be so unwise unless we are going to retreat from the world." [3]

A few days before in an address to the Protestant Council of the City of New York he had said that "the family of man could not long endure . . . this growing gulf between the rich and the poor."

> The rich must help the poor. The industrialized nations must help the developing nations . . .
> To weaken or water down the pending program, to confuse and confine its flexibility with rigid restrictions and rejections, will not only harm our economy, it will hamper our security.
> It will waste our present investment. And it will, above all, forfeit our obligations to our fellow man—obligations that stem from our wealth and strength, from our devotion to freedom and from our membership in the family of man.

And he reverted to earlier admonitions against discouragement and fatigue—admonitions that are among the memorials of his will and faith.

> Some say they are tiring of this task, or tired of world problems, or tired of hearing those who receive our aid disagree with our diplomacy. But what kind of spirit is that? Are we tired of living in a free world?
> Do we expect to make it over in our own image? Are we going to quit now because there are problems not yet solved? . . . Surely we are not going to throw away our hopes and means in an outburst of petty irritation and frustration.
> My fellow Americans . . . . Let us heed the words of Paul the

3. Press Conference, November 14, 1963. Transcript in *The New York Times,* November 15, 1963.

Apostle to the Galatians: "Let us not be weary in well-doing for in due season we shall reap, if we faint not." [4]

The recent droop in support of the foreign aid program does not indicate that the United States is less determined to combat Communism. But it does denote doubts about the efficacy of foreign aid as a weapon in the struggle. It is causing keener and more critical examination of the three connected sets of suppositions and inferences on which has rested this prime justification for foreign aid.

The first supposition is that the discontent of nations living in poverty has become so acute that they will barter with anyone for the means of satisfying their desires and pay with political favors and support. This is deemed especially possible in the case of newly independent nations which believe that, since they were kept down as colonies, the Western countries which in the past throve on their labor and resources now have an obligation to aid them, either as recompense or from penitence. The resultant inference is that unless the United States (as well as the other capitalist countries) gives them all needed assistance, and without asking anything in return, the Communist bloc, by taking advantage of the resultant resentment, will win influence and allies.

The second connected supposition is that the United States (and other capitalist countries) can and must convince the impoverished peoples that they need not adopt Communism or acquiesce in its ways to achieve economic growth and social justice. The Soviet Union and China must be shown up as oppressive and inefficient models of the mechanisms of material improvement as compared with those of the Western industrial countries—which leave room for individual initiative and respect individual rights and ambitions.

The third supposition is more subtle. As set forth by Walt Whitman Rostow, head of the Policy Planning Staff in the State Department, in a speech in February 1962: "The Communists also

4. *The New York Times,* November 9, 1963.

perceive that the process of modernization involves fundamental social, political and economic change. These are bound to be turbulent times; and it is the Communist intent to exploit the turbulence of this transition process in order to seize power and to mold the emerging world in their image and link it tightly to the Communist Empire." Thus, he suggested that Communism should be viewed and dealt with as ". . . a disease of the transitional process . . . which well-trained, well-organized professional cadres seek to impose on societies at the early stages of their modernization."

Such dismaying versions of the reasons why economic aid must be provided for all poor and aspiring foreign countries if Communism is not to prevail, have caused many Americans to think of themselves as living in a stockade with danger on every side, with great risks in whatever strategy of aid is pursued. If we do *not* do our utmost to help those who are no longer fain to live in stagnant poverty they may well resort to Communism in the hope of changing their lives. However, if we *do* use our resources and knowledge to propel and lead rapid change, there is the risk that the resultant dislocations will give Communist agitators and organizers a good opportunity to gain control.

Both hazards do exist. As Eugene Black has pointed out: "Economic development is a fickle process; it destroys old habits and attitudes toward life, even as it creates the wherewithal for a better material life; it creates human desires often too much faster than it provides for the means of its gratification; its one continual and over-riding requirement is change; by itself it leads nowhere in particular and may lead anywhere in general." [5]

Neither in a condition of resigned misery nor in one of feverish effort to get ahead is a nation immune from the virus of Communism. Even when a nation is making headway and knows it, Communist indoctrinators still can find causes to espouse, angers to incite, wrongs to exaggerate, envies and hatreds to exploit. By

5.   Eugene R. Black, *The Diplomacy of Economic Development,* page 19.

doing so, they may attract followers not only in quiescent societies but also in progressing ones that are still discontented and divided. However, they have thus far managed to win out only when the patient was racked and miserable, as were Russia and China at the end of long and devastating wars.

The United States has wisely chosen the positive strategy and accepted the risks of thrusting nations into the dangerous straits of economic and social transition. It could not now reverse this course even though it should wish to do so. It must not waver in the belief that economic and social progress will give political freedom and private economic initiative—not Communism—the better chance.

Behind and elevating the American struggle against international Communism is the hope that foreign aid will also be one of the preliminary steps toward the lasting pacification of the society of nations.

Present hopes of preserving the peace rest on one or both of two kindred expectations. One is that if the United States and its associates continue to increase and display their combined power, the "cold war" will be won; the Communist countries will either break up or quarrel among themselves; and in either case they will cease to be a great danger. The other is that even if this does not come about, the Communist bloc—convinced that it cannot defeat the West by propaganda, superiority of performance, conspiracy or terror—will come to acceptable terms.

To permit myself an interjection; this policy is conceived to be defensive and governed by the wish to protect ourselves without war. Most Western historians would adjudge it to have been mainly so up to now, and I agree with them. However, the policy must be kept under critical scrutiny. For it would be wondrous if American officials, like those of other governments, did not now and again overstep the reasonable rims of national self-protection. The boundary between defense and offense is hard to determine in advance. Many measures have both defensive and offensive effects. So that actually what must be sought is a balance rather than a boundary. Some officials do not drill themselves in close and candid inspection of their purposes. Others may lack the knowledge or insight to judge the effect of their acts or utterances. Thus the American public must continue to encourage inquisitive and independent minds to question, criticize, and say what they think. One reason why the Soviet Union has transgressed so often is that questioning and opposition are not allowed in that country.

Whatever the route taken, most Americans hope that this cold war in which they are using foreign aid will turn out to be just a long and trying passage toward a transformed international situation. They are desirous that the present abominable contest that is dividing the world be replaced by a reconciled society of nations which will have renounced recourse to war, and are willing to rely on peaceful procedures to adjust rivalries and settle disputes.

This is the ultimate aim which most Americans would like their foreign aid to serve. They are in accord with the avowal made by Secretary of State Rusk, when discussing the then proposed Foreign Assistance Act of 1962 with the Senate Committee on Foreign Relations:

> (Our commitment) is basically the structure that is outlined in the opening portions of the United Nations Charter—a world society of independent states, freely cooperating across national frontiers in pursuit of common interests upon which they are agreed. So that if one was to ask us what our primary target is in the international scene, I would say a family of independent states in a cooperative relation with each other.[6]

Despite the evident limits of the effectiveness of the United Nations up to now, most American people still look to that grouping of nations to translate this vision into reality. They remain faithful to the principles of the United Nations and convinced that it is indispensable as an agency for discussion and conciliation.

6. Hearings, April 5, 1962, pages 25–26.

But at present they are assailed by doubts whether the poor countries whom they assist will increase or decrease the serviceability of the United Nations as a peace agency. Will the many nations now living in poverty and privation care enough about war or peace, life or death? Will they reject calls to hate the more fortunate and explanations of their plight which place the blame on others? Will they be much concerned over the remoter consequences of any bargain they may make with the Communist bloc in return for help? By its aid programs the American people hope to shape the responses of the recipients to these and related questions.

Along with the wish for peace is a sense of responsibility for some of the new nations which have expelled their imperial governors. Having witnessed the dissolution of the British, French, Belgian and Dutch Empires with equanimity, the American government is now worried lest the newly emerged countries slump into misery and cruel disorder, or be beguiled by Communist diatribes and promises. The joint letter which Secretary of State Rusk and Secretary of the Treasury Dillon sent to members of Congress on July 19, 1961, urging approval of the submitted foreign aid program is a typical expression of that worry:

> With respect to economic assistance, nations old and new are struggling along the path of formal independence to nationhood and are determined to have the benefits of modern civilization. If the democratic world does not help them, the Communists will leap aboard this revolution of freedom, seize it, direct it to their own ends, and make it the instrument of their limitless imperialist ambitions.

In dealing with these countries, including even some whose leaders quote Thomas Jefferson, Thomas Paine, and Woodrow Wilson, the United States still suffers from a distorted image of itself—that of a grasping imperialist country. The American people have a right to be indignant at the accusation and the need to keep on refuting it. For since 1914 the United States passed up, without even taking much trouble to call attention to its self-restraint, several easy chances to become a great colonial power. Yet the fact remains—those who have a grudge against us or dislike our ways and institutions, or who think that by spewing hate and contempt upon the United States they can elevate themselves into power, have managed to keep alive the idea that it is the exemplar of oppressive imperialism. They decry the interest shown by the American government in the treatment of American enterprises, likening it to the imperialist intrusions of the past. They allege that doctrinaire defenses of private enterprise and profit prove our inhumanity.

The American government has been trying zealously to destroy this image once and for all, everywhere. Perhaps too zealously, for a misleading impression may have been given of readiness to see all former colonies through the hardships of their first years of self-government and of inexhaustible indulgence toward their faults and criticisms.

It should be noted, albeit briefly, that American power to provide financial or economic aid has been used as an accompaniment to an effort to forfend against impending wars between other countries or to end wars between them in which the United States might be involved. There have been several critical emergencies which might have brought on great wars, if one or several of the wealthier nations had not aided the adversaries while they were being separated and calmed down, and thereafter provided the means to keep open the chance of a peaceable settlement. This is the reason why the United States has been supporting the Arab refugees from Palestine and their progeny, the Central government of the Congo, the coalition government in Laos, and the huge project to put to joint use the great rivers of the Indus Basin that run through India and Pakistan.

These and other diverse purposes that animate American programs of foreign aid are basically congruent. As a nation we invest, lend, give, instruct, rescue and resuscitate needy peoples in the belief that it will advantage our national security and reputation as well as our souls. Yet—yet, those who are helped must be kept aware that the United States is not ultimately dependent on their favor. Its activities in aid must not be deformed or rotted by fright. Americans want associates in order to end those tensions which sunder the whole wide world—to end them by mutual toleration—time-tempering toleration—rather than by trial in battle. They would like all nations, large or small, to have a fair chance to improve their conditions of life and work, in orderly freedom, without compulsion from outside or social strife within. These should be, if they are not, the messages conveyed by the clangor of foreign aid.

Yet the United States must not ever assume that its economic aid in and of itself can assure friendship or even reliable impartiality. The deployment of American economic power will not in itself do so if our character deteriorates; if our life is gashed by divisions between blacks and whites, workers and employers, city and country. Or if we do not maintain armed forces strong enough to cause enemies to pause. Or if our diplomacy lacks suppleness, reasonableness, and appeal. Our willingness to help must be a symbol of health and virtues, not a signal of dependence on others.

7 | The Assumed Assignment

While listening to statements of what we aim to achieve by foreign aid, the spirit is uplifted. But the spirit may sag when the panorama of poverty we would like to relieve is envisioned. The area of destitution is vast and striated.

The vista is smudged by sight of the so many dreadful human situations that have so long persisted. The dark, dank existence in the charcoal and fishing villages of Brazil; the shivering and dull-eyed Indians in the mountain towns of Peru, Bolivia, and Ecuador; the huddled destitution in Sicily intensified by searing tempers and cruel violence; the teeming half-starved millions in the dirt and dung of the congested villages and city slums in India, the sickly and hungry jute redders of East Pakistan and the refugees from India huddled in the hovels of Dacca; the teeming, ignorant millions in the tropical villages of Java; the ragged, sickly workers along the Nile, and the beggarly families in the back streets of Cairo; the pestilential, rotting, vermin-infested quarters and alleys in Morocco and Algiers; the ignorant weird congregations in tribal villages and eroded hillsides of tropical Africa; the sadness and blindness of children in the fly-blown tenements of Bagdad, Tabriz and Teheran; the displaced families trudging over dusty, bleak roads of Korea, or squatting in smoky huts.

For them and their brothers and sisters in other lands (more than a billion, and fifty million more human beings each year, not counting those on the mainland of China) flood, drought, aridity, disease, war, harmful sensual practices, misrule and oppression, the biological urge, corruption and chronic political turmoil, customs suppressive of effort, any of the infinite combinations of these and other misery-makers, have been too much. In the past most of them have lived in fear or hopelessness. They have tried to propitiate fate while praying for a savior.

But now their desire and expectation are changing. The belief that they can better themselves and cure their sicknesses and educate their children has spread far and fast. This has been aroused by the spread of knowledge of what can be done by modern technology. It has been furthered by both Communist propaganda and the optimistic advertising of the West—hurtling into distressed bodies and ignorant minds. Most of the newly wishful and hopeful do not ask themselves whether they have the means and abilities to achieve their desires. Nor do they consider whether they are willing to submit to the disciplines and make the exertions by which they might do so.

This is the surge of aspiration with which American diplomacy has to reckon as it pursues, through the extension of foreign aid, its many purposes. How sensible has the United States been to engage its good faith and fortune in this cause?

The historical record is sobering. It tells over and over again of the ills for which economic aid is no lasting corrective. Advocates and agents of foreign aid have been compelled to recognize this grim reality. Some have turned pessimists. Others have become better instructors of the people they want to help; sterner and more reproving perhaps, but less likely to mislead either the seekers or suppliers of aid by specious forecasts. Few expositors still write and talk as though they believe that lasting material improvement can be assured merely by providing external resources, capital and technical aid. These may be crucial for achieving it, but they do not guarantee that it will be achieved.

Such being the assignment to which the American government is addressing itself, let us take a closer look at what must be attempted. I enumerate merely to identify, not to indicate priorities or connections.

First, to act on the Confucian belief that knowledge and action are integrally linked. A literate, suitably educated people will be able to do much more for itself than will an ignorant one. It is more likely to attract desirable immigration. It will be more able to buy, borrow, beg or steal techniques and to secure foreign capital, than will an ignorant one even though its character and resources are no better.

Hence, the American government as well as many private institutions are responding to requests to instruct poorer peoples in the elements of literacy and in the skills needed in industry, agriculture, government and the professions. Some of our aid programs contemplate only the temporary visitation of scores of Americans and others to give them primary instruction in reading, writing, arithmetic, hygiene and geography. Other programs include arrangements for training and qualifying hundreds either in their home countries, in the United States or elsewhere or semi-skilled jobs in industry, construction, road building, farming and business administration. Others enable ever-growing numbers of more advanced and tested students to continue their studies in liberal arts colleges, technical and agricultural institutions, medical, law and engineering schools. The United States is holding back no book or branch of knowledge because the task of instruction may prove too onerous.

This diffusion of education is a wager on the belief that literate and trained peoples will not only be capable of improving their conditions but will also choose to associate with the Western non-Communist world of "voluntarism." Some may not. Assisted education may fashion ideas and attitudes that will be harmful to the educators. Those who are taught to read and write, under electric lighting supplied by American capital and technicians, may the more rapidly absorb Communist propaganda in newspapers, tracts and pamphlets. A populace that has learned just enough to know the ways of living in the more affluent countries may come to envy and hate rather than to emulate them. Thus, our ability to convince others of the virtues of a form of free and self-respecting society must surpass our effort to educate.

The tempo and kinds of higher education should be a little in advance of the requirements of each community but not too far in advance. One desirable effect of providing better educational opportunity may be the re-direction of the interests and energies of students from political agitation to the tasks of learning. But it is futile to train large numbers to make a livelihood in trade or business unless the chances of their doing so are at the same time being expanded. Enough men and women should be instructed in the law, medicine, engineering and other professions to leaven and lead the community but not more than can make careers in the country.

Caution should restrain encouragement of eager young men and women to aspire to be lawyers, civil servants, judges, democratic political leaders unless their country is on the way toward adopting systems of government, law and administration in which they may serve with professional pride. For, as pointed out by Eugene Black in his book, *The Diplomacy of Economic Development:* "There is no more explosive political material than the doctor who knows what modern medicine can do but does not have the facilities to put his knowledge to work; or the teacher who must teach, if at all, without textbooks; or the engineer without access to capital equipment; or the businessman without a place of business; or the politician without a following who knows what he is talking about." Or, to add to Black's enumeration, the reporter who cannot find a newspaper to print the news he has found out, the competent author who cannot find a publisher or a public, or the architect who cannot get jobs, instructors of literature, political science, history, economics, anthropology and biology who cannot secure university posts, or naval officers without ships, army officers without divisions, pilots without planes. All in such frustrating circumstances may be tempted to believe they will fare better under another government or a different form of government.

Second, to help countries regenerate natural resources that have been spoiled or neglected; and to enable them to deal more ably with the trials of nature—drought, flood, extreme heat and cold, predatory insects, overbearing jungles, poor soil, high mountains.

Third, to teach peoples what they must do to keep well, to build up their energies, and to take care of the sick; and to provide the means by which this can be done.

Better health increases the capacity to work and push ahead. The prospect of longer life arouses the will to learn and to struggle against the miserliness or caprices of physical environment. However, public health projects may have cancelling consequences of which notice will be taken later.

Fourth, to persuade those who want to emerge from poverty to master unfounded fears; to cast off harmful superstitions and legends; and to amend attitudes and loyalties which, expressed in customs and laws, lessen both the incentive to work and the result of work.

Fifth, to convince people that they must deny themselves goods and pleasures today so that they can accumulate the means of increasing what they may enjoy tomorrow.

Sixth, to encourage and enable people, while governing themselves, to correct social and political inequalities and injustices. In striving to do so, hard problems are being met. While the poor masses must benefit enough to support the national effort, those who are capable of directing production must be well rewarded, and those who have larger fortunes and incomes must be induced to save and invest. To effect and keep a balance between these several aims, official powers may have to be strenuously used. Governments of countries in the throes of reform can never relax.

Seventh, to accustom people to submit to the disciplines and constraints of systematized farming and industry.

Eighth, to influence people in so far as possible, to abide peaceably within rules of law and order.

If such are the requisites for bringing about material improvement, then those engaged in the efforts *must* act not only as donors and technical advisers but also as animators, tutors, moralists and monitors. Experience has upset the belief that unfortunate nations need *only* a strong helping hand—or arm—or shovel—to make their way forward. The American authorities and people have learned that readiness to provide these aids is only the preliminary condition for carrying on the set task. They have found out how much more has to be done and how much more retarded countries must be called on to do—not least to endure the dislocations and strains of change. The United States must expect at times to be sorely tried, to be denigrated and fooled by some of those it seeks to help.

After this delineation of the scope and multiple elements of the assignment, I wish to inject a warning against approaching it with uniform and rigid standards. Statistical measurements of the conditions to be corrected, and of the projected rate of material improvement ought not to be the sole meters or arbiters of our policy. Increases in indices of physical production—tons of steel, kilowatts of electricity, yards of cloth, numbers of new houses—or in monetary measurement—usually the Gross National Product—are certainly significant indicators of success or failure. But how are they to be equated with the pleasure of being idle in the sun, of taking days off to fish or hunt or visit, with the amusement of playing with small children, or the satisfaction of the slow rhythm of planting by hand rather than by machine, or with the companionability of family work in the fields, or with the pleasures of polygamy that many have praised? I do not know. Such inclinations and practices must be kept in check if people are to progress economically. But how firmly are suppliers of aid to combat them, how unconditionally condemn all resistance to submission to the exacting terms of greater productivity?

What informed surmises support the belief that the many needed innovations can be brought about? Not everywhere, of course, nor quickly, nor without interruption and relapse, but in so great a measure that American purposes in making the effort and bearing the expense will be well served. Those who believe this can be done point to the great material progress made by many countries during the past century. Looking ahead they can point to the large margin of capital which the more affluent countries can now spare to help the poorer, if they so will, and to the amassed stock of knowledge, inventions and fabrications which they can supply.

The pace and possibilities of transfer of productive knowledge is much more rapid than in former times. What was encompassed in centuries in the long past may be done now in decades. Before the Western world attained its present leadership in economic development there was a nurturing period of several centuries, a long period of absorption and adjustment. Truly observed by that eminent student of economic history, Simon Kuznets: "The leadership today of the Western world in modern economic development . . . is an outcome of a long process of learning from its more advanced neighbors in the Near and Far East; but the intellectual, political and geographical revolutions which occurred between the 13th and 16th centuries were important and indispensable antecedents to the economic expansion that followed." [1] But the revolutions have speeded up in our time and the technical and many more capital-creating antecedents for similar advances in the rest of the world are in existence now. The deeper uncertainty now is whether the people of the poorer countries are willing and able to qualify themselves to use these means of material improvement, and whether their political and social situation will allow them to do so.

1. *Underdeveloped Countries and the Pre-industrial Phase in the Advanced Countries.* Proceedings of the World Population Conference, 1954 Papers, Volume V.

In the fact that poverty, like prosperity, may be self-perpetuating and cumulative the believers see a reason for hope. In some cases it may be due to irremediable defects of character and conduct or insuperable natural environment. But the causes of poverty tend to create a vicious circle perpetuating themselves and the state of poverty. Certainly the failure of many nations in the past may be due in part to what Ragnar Nurske has called "a circular constellation of forces tending to act and react upon one another in such a way as to keep a poor country in a state of poverty." [2] The proffered exposition of the way in which this chain of linked consequences runs, although oversimplified, seems to me tenable as a working hypothesis, ". . . a poor man may not have enough to eat; being undernourished, his health may be weak; being physically weak, his working capacity may be low, which means he is poor, which in turn means that he will not have enough to eat; and so on." In these and other ways stagnant poverty may be self-perpetuating and self-reinforcing. In a country where little is going on, where routine is unbroken, where purchasing power is small, effort will be half-hearted. Many are unable to get work, or only part-time or seasonal work. Trained men and women will seek better chances for themselves elsewhere. The country will lose its more able commercial leaders, farmers, managers of production and technicians. Natural resources will be neglected and spoiled.

When these conditions prevail the proposition that "a country is poor because it is poor" is partially a valid observation not merely a redundant witticism. And if that is so, if the circle of causation is broken at several points for a long enough time, will not the country progress? Does that not give solid ground for faith in the relieving power of foreign assistance, and even in the probability that progress may be self-propelling? A state of brisk activity, offering work to all, will stimulate a wish for the rewards of

2. Ragnar Nurske, *Some Aspects of Capital Accumulation in Undeveloped Countries*, Cairo, 1952. For a variant presentation see his *Problems of Capital Formation in Underdeveloped Countries*. Oxford, 1953.

work and foster habits of work. True, sometimes greater ease and the certainty of having work may cause men and women to labor less steadily than they would if their meals and shelter were always in hazard. The prospect of assured employment may have this effect when wants are few and simple and there is no spur to greater effort than is necessary to satisfy them. Or where the climate is so debilitating that all exertions except those that must be made to get along from day to day are avoided. Or where the conditions in mines or factories are so disagreeable, strange and lonely that workers will quit as soon as they can. But, to repeat, in most poor countries the acceleration of activity will have a tonic effect. The chance to get work and advance one's self will arouse and strengthen the wish and willingness to work.

Besides these broad reasons for the view that poverty can be rapidly reduced if the minimum means for a fair start are provided and the conditioning terms are met, others no less conjectural may be adduced. Small additional amounts of capital and accruals of knowledge can have a greater productive potential in poor and undeveloped countries than in the more advanced ones. The introduction of even slightly more efficient means and methods into a primitive system can have a higher proportionate and quicker impact on productivity than in the countries already utilizing superior ones. Figuratively speaking, a small application of aid can exert more force in hauling one country out of the depths than in elevating another to a higher station.

This supposition finds support in simple observed instances. The use of cheap sprays and chemicals that drive away hordes of sand flies and horse flies can change the whole tempo of life and work in an area. The drilling of a few wells, better ways of lining them to retain water, and the installations of a few small pumps can transform parched land. Industrial workers can do much more at home and in the factory if they can come and go on bicycles rather than on foot or in bullock carts. What a difference it can make to have electric power to turn the lathes in small furniture work-shops, to turn the grinding wheels in small cutlery shops! How much more effectively the farmer can work in his fields if he has a metal plow with a moldboard, and a mattock to dig up roots; the man clearing land for a home if he has a power saw; the fisherman if his boat has an outboard motor; the tanner if he has a circular cutting knife to use on hides and skins and a good drying stand! These are a few examples of the thousands of simple and inexpensive innovations that can greatly change the condition of a village or a town within a few years, if social and political arrangements do not stand in the way of their effective use.

The introduction of easily mastered techniques, tools, small engines and machines, electric power and chemical treatments may add more to the productivity of workers and land in hotter countries than those in temperate zones. It is probable, for example, that in a tropical country the use of a power mower will count more, will do the work of more men, than in a temperate country where men can use scythes without exhaustion. The productive value of a power-saw in a tropical country in clearing away vegetation and holding back the jungle will exceed what it could be in a more temperate climate.

To these surmises and the examples used to illustrate them, there must be appended the pointed reminder of Lynn White: ". . . a new device merely opens a door; it does not compel one to enter. The acceptance or rejection of an invention, or the extent to which its implications are realized if it is accepted, depends quite as much on the condition of a society, and upon the imagination of its leaders, as upon the nature of the technological item itself." [3]

Lacking the traits of dynamism, the state of the people of Imperial China (who, more inventive than Europeans a thousand years ago, first printed with movable type and used explosives, the magnetic compass, wind gauges, seismoscopes and the screw),

3. Lynn White, Jr., *Medieval Technology and Social Change*, page 28.

changed for the worse while the Western world pulsated and expanded.[4]

These are all persuasive reasons for the belief that the task which the American people have taken upon themselves is manageable in satisfactory measure. They allow the hope that the roughly defined range of objectives of the American foreign aid program can be achieved by many, if not most, countries now living in grave poverty. What is thought to be feasible is an annual cumulative increase in gross national product of about four per cent, of which half may be required by many of the assisted countries to take care of their growing population.

However, any bold commitment must rest on faith, not on predictive certainty. Knowing this, and still being determined not to falter, let us observe with open eyes and minds some of the main hindrances which may defeat faith and condemn peoples to poverty and suffering despite the wish to aid them.

4. Article by Caryl P. Haskins in *Foreign Affairs,* January 1962, "Science and Foreign Policy."

8 | The Hindrances

Of all the hindrances to cooperation for economic growth one is, I believe, the hardest to surmount. This is the fact that many of the peoples who most need capital—counsel—education—technical instruction—are of different skin color than those who can provide most of them.

This may adversely affect the inclination to be generous of an affluent country peopled by whites. Or it may be the basis for the belief that the poorer people of darker skin will not be able to progress rapidly or steadily, and therefore help must be carefully measured and its uses controlled. Or it may even arouse fear or misgiving that the supplier will later come to regret having nursed peoples of other colors.

Conversely it may affect the inclinations of needy countries to accede even to essential terms and conditions of assistance. It may cause them to resist orders intended to carry out even approved purposes; or to reject proposals which would subject them to control of white supervisors.

Even when it does not check the willingness to give and accept help in any of these ways, difference in color may be a bar to easy association between people of white skin and those of black, yellow or even brown skins. The sense of otherness is, I believe, reciprocal. Almost all the officials, executives and technicians from the white Western world who are engaged in helping the peoples of Africa, Asia and the Middle East are striving hard to ignore or overcome it. Continuous and pleasant association in work inspired by a shared purpose usually diminishes and may wholly eclipse the sense of separation. But that tendency is often checked by the fact that the mentors enjoy superior working and living conditions within the host country. Employed in higher capacities than most natives, they live more comfortably and their permanent interests and contacts lie in their own home countries. So all too often the sense of separation persists. The visitors do not feel at ease; they are seldom free of anxiety lest they give offense. Unknowingly they may give the impression that they feel superior because they are white. Unconscious signs that they do feel this way may be apparent only to those whose skin is black or yellow.

Mutual awareness of difference may prevent each from taking a detached view of the opinions of the other. Thus, foreign peoples of darker color may attribute to scorn or distaste any adverse or even cool comments on their ways or actions or beliefs. Just and necessary orders and reproofs by a white instructor or employer may be construed as due to color bias.

Akin to and often mingled with the alienation and strains caused by differences in color are those engendered by differences in racial affiliation. For our purpose we need not try to define racial variances in anthropological or biological terms or forms. Nor need we—nor could we—distinguish them from differences in nationality. Nor need we—nor could we—tell which may be fundamental and relatively permanent, and which merely environmental and fluid. Define races, classify them as you will—or as the experts will—the evinced differences often have a restraining effect on association and cooperation in aid programs. Who can deny that even persons of similar Western racial origins—for example, Americans, English, French, Germans and Italians—have to be more careful about what they do and say when living and working together than when they are with persons of their own group? How much more careful must they be when among Orientals, East

Indians, Arabs and Africans; and how much more watchful and inhibited must these in turn be in dealing with the foreigners of alien race.

Some students of the relations between peoples of different color and/or race attribute the breaches in communication to differences in status, education, ways of speech, incomes, memories, and the transmission of fear or prejudice from adults of one generation to the children of the next. I believe these to be at least part of the cause; they do accentuate and keep constantly to the fore the sense of otherness. Herein is ground for hope that the hindering effects of both color and race may be lessened when and as poorer peoples begin to better their material conditions, become more educated, and more alike in their ways of living and thinking to the more affluent peoples.

But during the period of transition, differences in color and race will handicap the efforts of many of the poorer peoples to better their condition. The natives of Asia, Africa and the Middle East have won their demand to be treated as equals by whites of European origin, to enjoy the same political rights, personal esteem and opportunities. They resent any show of patronage, assumptions of superiority and social aloofness. They want what the industrialized world has to give. But they will not acknowledge any right to expect subservience in return. However, some of the white suppliers, advisers, and tutors think themselves entitled to superior authority and privilege.

The strains may be more trying in countries that have recently become independent, for their people are still smarting from the experience of subordination. Their struggle for independence derived impetus from the determination to oust men of different color or race from positions of control and strip them of their assumed and, in the view of the former subject peoples, unmerited advantages. Some native aspirants for power or office in these countries will, as before, seek supporters by rekindling old grievances. When they do, the effect on the conduct of foreign aid programs is injurious. Such political behavior has caused setbacks in aid programs, for example, in Egypt, Algeria, Indonesia, Burma, Ceylon and Kenya.

I have only generalities to offer as to how this active, or latent, hindrance to effective cooperation for economic growth may be offset or eradicated. Both the helpers and the helped must make whatever emotional adjustments may be required to get on with the job. The helpers must take care not to give offense; the helped must be slow to take offense. By mutual toleration and respect they can live and work together satisfactorily even though they do not lose entirely their sense of otherness. The aloofness that was deemed necessary for command under imperial rule is now more likely to arouse opposition than enhance respect for leadership.

Fortunately, most countries greatly in need of help are apt to be stoical. If treated with manifest good will they generally put their needs above their feelings. Our aid program must be imbued by a sense of universality and heartfelt recognition of the common lot of mankind. For the job of surmounting differences of color and race will be made the harder by the delusive propaganda about "the brotherhood of men under Communism."

The differences of color and race and all others that separate those who need help from those who can help is all the more hurtful when physical conditions are adverse. Then greater joint effort is required for material improvement.

In the very hot countries scorching sun and extreme heat drain the body and deaden the mind. Who, enduring them, wants to work more than he must; more than just enough to get indispensable food and clothing, shelter from sun and rain and wind? What if, despite effort and care, torrential downpours leach the soil and wash out the seeds and roots, or prolonged drought parches the plants, or omnivorous insects devour them, or the jungle encroaches, or the wood in houses rots, the cement crumbles, the mud walls subside? Then is it not likely to seem sensible to reconcile himself to making do with very little rather than to try again and again?

In the northernmost cold regions, what if the growing season is too short, or strong winds blow down the crops, or snow and extreme cold kill the livestock, or much energy is needed just to keep warm? Then is it not likely to seem sensible either to attempt to do only what can surely withstand the weather, or to migrate?

Since the greatest disparities in economic condition are between countries in the temperate zones and those in the sub-tropical zones, some able students epitomize the problem of alleviation of poverty as a North-South one. In the past, climate (using that word to mean the whole physical environment) has often been the most salient and crucial cause of the extremes of disparity. But one does not have to look far to find instances that indicate that it has not always been so.

In our own times some peoples are doing much better than others in like physical conditions. There is much less poverty in Lebanon than in the neighboring countries. The Japanese and the Koreans live in similar climatic belts, yet one country has a far higher standard of living than the other. The Costa Ricans are getting along much better than the other Central American nations. How well the Scots have managed in their poorly endowed terrain, and how sturdily they have upheld themselves! What a prosperous country the Swiss have made of their mountain valleys and limpid lakes! I am chary about adding the Israelis to the list of exceptional performers because they have been so enormously helped from outside; but how many immigrants have been settled in that small and dry patch of territory, there to make for themselves an ardent personal and throbbing national life.

These instances do not disprove the great importance of physical environment in determining what a country may achieve materially. They merely indicate that adverse "climate" need not mean compulsory poverty. Certainly less so now than in earlier periods, since we have become far more able to contend against nature and offset the adverse effects of "climate". Many new ways and means of coping are being brought to bear. This is one of the main branches of the aid effort. Overflow of rivers can be controlled;

parched land irrigated; denuded slopes reforested; jungles bull-dozed; hills leveled; pests, parasites and plagues held in check.

Life in almost any climate can be made, and is being made, more tolerable by devices innumerable. Factories and offices and houses can be cooled or warmed; insects can be kept out or killed off; foods can be refrigerated and more quickly prepared and cooked; houses can be made more weatherproof, clothing more protective, roads easier to travel; communications quicker and surer, and entertainment and information can be conveyed everywhere by radio and television.

Similarly, work in any climate can be and is being made easier as well as more effective. Even the poorest peoples are now procuring some of the new kinds of tools and machines that assist and relieve their arms, backs and legs. And all forms of power—oil, gas, electric, atomic, are on the way toward them—bought, borrowed or donated; as are the small engines, pumps and motors that multiply energy and lessen the call on human exertion in harsh physical conditions.

This ranging survey of the obstacles to cooperation for economic growth may be indented at this point by more detailed comments on those problems which cluster about the use of the land and natural resources, since these impair the prospect of progress in so many poor countries. The problems differ, not only between countries, but between regions in the same country.

The usual pattern of ownership of land and its accessory rights may be faulty in any one or all of several ways.

In some of the more primitive regions, particularly in Africa, production is hindered by tribal ownership or control of arable and grazing lands, and of water rights. Each farmer may or may not be permitted to retain most of what he raises on the land he is given the right to cultivate. But since he cannot borrow on it or sell it, or pass it on as an inheritance, he does not exert himself to improve his allotment, save to buy tools, drill wells or drain seepage.

On timber lands held in common, cutting may be so heedless that the land erodes. If grazing rights are shared, each user is likely to lead his animals to the more fertile spots until these are gone; goats are allowed to eat the young shoots until the land is barren and the top soil is washed away. When the water supply is limited and held in common, unless it is measured out among all those who have a claim upon it, use is apt to be careless and wasteful.

Where communal ownership stunts production, American influence should be used to define, confirm and sometimes reassert individual rights. But the basic system of taking care of all members of the group should not be abruptly smashed.

In other countries, notably in Latin America and the Middle East, production is smaller than it should be, even with the local methods of production, because so much of the good farming or grazing areas is owned by a small number of wealthy families. Some of their large farms and ranches are managed well, others are run neglectfully. Some proprietors leave much of their spacious realms fallow. Around each of them there may be several sorts of wretched dependencies whose people work for the principal owner. These laborers have little or no chance of acquiring parcels of land of their own. To do so has become a burning desire to satisfy which the peasant families in many countries will, if necessary, resort to direct action or revolution. For, as observed in one of the reports of a Sub-Committee of the Joint Economic Committee of Congress on Economic Conditions in South America:

> To the campesino (worker on the land) ownership of the land is more than a source of wealth. It is the source of prestige and political power and social justice. . . . It lets him share in the bundle of rights which have so long been the prerogative of the large landowner and denied to the landless. . . . The landless see in ownership of a piece of land a kind of job protection and assurance that, whatever happens, they will have food and shelter. . . . Through land ownership the landless hope for status in their communities, freedom to act and speak freely, the opportunity to

see their children given an education, and the right to share in control over their government.[1]

Where concentration of ownership retards production while swelling discontent, the American government should be predisposed to favor plans to apportion the land among many smaller working farmers, either individually or collectively. It can support its advice by offers to cooperate with local authorities in aiding and instructing the new proprietors.

In some countries, the problem is just the opposite. Because of law or custom the division of ownership has gone too far. Many family holdings are so small or scattered that the better methods and means of cultivation cannot be used and the product is meager. When this is so, policy must be directed toward exchanges of land and consolidation into units large enough for better farming. Laws of inheritance may have to be amended. As these and other measures to the same end may lessen the number of those who are needed on the land, their introduction should be related to the prospect that those who are displaced can find other self-supporting work. Otherwise, while total product grown on the land may increase, so will unemployment, discontent, and both rural and urban destitution.

Even when the division of ownership is suitable to the nature of the area and methods of farming, the title may be insecure. This may be either because of uncertainty in the laws affecting land titles or because laws are not administered impartially. When farmers know they can be ousted by those who enjoy official favor or have powerful family or financial connections, or if the landlord can make a better bargain, they will not try hard to improve the land and add to their farm equipment. The nature of the remedy needed is indicated by the nature of the cause.

As consequential as any other bar to more production in some countries are the prevailing terms on which land is *rented*. If ten-

1. Report of the Subcommittee of Joint Economic Committee of Congress on Economic Conditions in South America, 1962, pages 6–7.

ants are required to turn over to landlords too large a share of the product, their work will be like that of prisoners serving a sentence for a pittance rather than that of free men trying to build a home around a livelihood. If they are not protected by law against excessive requisitions, they will be hesitant to do more than they must to keep from being thrown out by the landowner. The terms of tenancy should give enough incentive to work, plan and save. A fair prospect of being able to earn enough to buy the land, and an explicit option to do so are most conducive to its best use.

Another reason why the yield secured from the land in many poorer countries is less than it might be, even under existing laws and methods of cultivation, is that neither owners nor tenants can get credit at reasonable terms. The rates of interest demanded are exorbitant and/or the borrower is required to mortgage unconditionally his land, tools, machines—the whole substance of his living. Then the poor tenant or owner hit by bad weather or calamity will lose everything. Since the penalty of default on the payment of interest or repayment of borrowed money is so grave, prudent farmers, though skilled and energetic, will refrain from borrowing to extend their operations, or to buy machinery or fertilizer. When credit is not procurable on moderate terms the output of the farms is repressed, and better methods of farming are neglected.

In some countries and regions the product gained by work and investment on the land is less than it might be because owners and tenants are not cooperating with each other in ways that would benefit all. Often by entering into cooperative arrangements, and only by so doing, is it possible for small farmers to have an ample or regular supply of water, cheap fertilizer, protection against pests, the use of machines that individual farmers could not afford to buy or maintain, and facilities for storing food for animals. Nor can they, except by joining together, have their products satisfactorily processed—their grapes turned into wine, their livestock into meat, their wheat into flour, their standing timber into lumber and their lumber into pulp, their rice-straw into packing materials or mats, their vegetables packed for frozen packets or in cans; nor can they have their products brought as regularly into market for sale. By forming cooperatives, small farmers can do many things that otherwise they would be unable to do or to do as cheaply and well.

The scant return extracted from the land in some of the poorer countries is due to the fact that farmers, because of ignorance, custom or necessity, are making wrong use of their acres. They are striving to grow products which the soil or climate does not favor instead of those which would thrive. By demonstration of other possibilities, farmers can usually be led to change the use of their land—if they can be fairly sure they will be able to grow enough of the foods on which they live and find a market for the surplus. It is easier to bring about a redirection of effort than a reformation of property ownership or social structures in rural regions.

And lastly, the conditions of rural workers may be tipped toward poverty because of the absence of auxiliary occupations that can be carried on in the household or outside; supplementary earnings that can enable them to eke out a decent livelihood.

In these brief notes I have skirted a basic question, or rather taken the answer for granted. It is whether the people, in any or many of the poorer countries, may not do better under a system of state ownership of the land and its equipment, rather than under a system of private ownership and/or voluntary cooperation. Depending on random reading of others who have given the subject career-long attention, I make bold to offer a few observations.

One is that private ownership, rather widely distributed, is likely to be the most proficient basis for production of most food crops and natural fibers, especially those raised in the temperate zones. It almost certainly will be if titles of ownership are secure, terms of tenancy just, taxes moderate, credit cheap and accessible, instruction in better methods of farming available, and if it is supplemented by cooperative arrangements. Contemporary experience has been corroborating the same basic reason that impressed itself on William Bradford, the first Governor of the settlement in Plymouth, Massachusetts, in 1620:

> All this whille no supply was heard of, neither knew they when they might expecte any. So they begane to thinke how they might raise as much corne as they could, and obtaine a better crope than they had done, that they might not still thus languish in miserie. At length, after much debate of things, the Governor (with ye advice of ye cheefest amongst them) gave way that they should set corne every man for his owne particuler, and in that regard trust to them selves; in all other things to goe on in ye generall way as before. As so assigned to every family a parcell of land, according to the proportion of their number for that end, only for present use (but made no division for inheritance), and ranged all boys and youth under some familie. This had very good success; for it made all hands very industrious, so as much more corne was planted then otherwaise would have bene by any means ye Govr or any other could use, and saved him a great deal of trouble and gave farr better contente. The women now wente willingly into ye feild, and tooke their litle-ons with them to set corne, which before would aledg weaknes, and inabilitie; whom to have compelled would have bene thought great tiranie and oppression.
>
> The experience that was had in this comone course and condition, tried sundrie years, and that amongst godly and sober men, may well evince the vanitie of that conceite of Plato & other ancients, applauded by some of later times;—that ye taking away of propertie, and bringing in comunitie into a comone wealth, would make them happy and florishing; as if they were wiser then God.[2]

But production on an extensive and larger scale is more efficient for some foodstuffs such as coffee and sugar, and even for cereals and vegetables where the lay and character of the land permit use of huge machines, and for raw materials like timber and rubber. These can be grown and harvested so much more cheaply on large tracts by owners who have enough capital to employ costly equipment and use the best methods of irrigation, drainage and protection against pests and blight, and to standardize the quality of

2. *Report on the Disadvantages of Common Store*, by William Bradford.

their product, that the small farm—known as the family farm—cannot compete.

Even though that is so, in countries where many people could not find employment away from the land, the wiser course would be to support the small farmer and check the emergence of the huge farm, plantation or ranch. Decentralization of ownership of land and productive effort around the large directing and purchasing centers and of cooperation should be encouraged and sometimes imposed by law. The total resultant product will not be as great as if the tendency toward largeness were allowed free leeway. But the country may be better off if it enables greater numbers to participate in production on a small scale rather than have them become unskilled, drifting and often out-of-work laborers on great farms or in factories and cities. In this whole area of agricultural organization and tuition, the United States has much to give, along with whatever financial and technical help it may extend.

There is one other way in which flow of people into overcrowded cities and regions may be reduced. In many poor countries there are extensive areas of good land that could be opened up to farmers who are eager to own land. But this usually necessitates the construction of new roads, new clearing away of forest or jungle, housing, drainage or irrigation, instruction in individual and cooperative use of the added acreage. Such undertakings are costly. Sometimes qualified farmers cannot be induced to migrate into the strange neighborhood. Thus the chances of waste and failure in opening up new areas for farming are not small. Yet I believe the American government would be well-advised to look with favor on all such possibilities and be as ready to finance promising ones as it is to finance new industries.

Admittedly, even though people in want are helped to make much better use of their labor on the land, many of them may remain on or very close to the poverty line. This has engendered the conclusion that most of the poor countries that are now mainly dependent on the produce of the field or forest or sub-soil can make fast headway only by industrialization. The political leaders and economists have become convinced that they must establish local manufactures in which the fabulous new techniques and machines turn out the goods required for health and comfort, and the capital equipment for agriculture, industry and construction.

This bent of judgment and purpose is a sound one for most countries over the longer run. However, the early effects of the introduction of the new industries or rapid expansion in construction can be upsetting unless curbed or redressed by the community. News of novel activity may excite a rush into the industrial areas of many more people than can find therein work or a place to live —of men and women who are fleeing from rural regions where work is unremitting, returns small, days and nights dull and dark, unrelieved by hope or enlivened by change.

These refugees from the poor and sometimes sinister countryside have no gleaming aluminum mobile homes with electrical kitchens, as have the travelling families in the United States; nor any reserve of cash in the bank or in the pocket; nor families on whom to fall back; nor skills to offer; nor friends in the neighborhood; nor are there well-laid-out trailer camps or even tent colonies in which they can settle. For shelter they must scrabble for loose lumber, discarded tin sheeting, or make walls and roofs from mud and rubble. The squalid urban slums in which they just manage to keep alive from day to day disfigure the towns and cities and are a menace to health and order. Too many of the factory and commercial centers that have recently risen fast out of the mud or clay are ringed with such unhealthy and rotting shanty towns. Look out of almost any window in Bombay, Poona, Karachi, Jakarta, Rio de Janeiro, Caracas, Cali and you will see them.

David Lilienthal's observation of what occurred in the provincial capital of Ahwáz in Southeast Iran, as work upon a nearby major power and construction development went forward, conveys in essentials the causes of many similar hegiras into "the promised land" where factories are rising.

Cars are beginning to jam the streets. . . . On the city's outskirts new factories are being developed, there are more houses and a web of electric lines is bringing light to even old adobe settlements.

Word of these changes has passed . . . even to remote villages and out-of-the-way trading posts—places where, for centuries, the chief event was the slow passage of a tribe of nomads with their sheep, goats, donkeys and camels. And the rural people are swarming in Ahwáz—Arab families from the Iraqi border regions, impoverished young countrymen, tribesmen in full caravan. They come for jobs, for trade, because a crop has failed, or perhaps simply to see a spectacle. . . . In the farm villages . . . life is not only hard and bitter; it is spiritually deadening. . . . The lively city—despite its slums and shanty towns, despite the brutality and wickedness that breed in mass poverty—is better than the dead village.

But . . . , the great migration is creating acute social tensions. As the poor move to the cities, they swell the forces of a new urban class. The members of this class may live in shacks; they may lack pure water, medical facilities and schools for their children. If they are lucky they may have a few of the humbler decencies of life—a tiny plot of land for a house, a weekly visit by a municipal nurse, perhaps a regular distribution of flour.

Whatever their condition, once they are in a city they can measure their own lot against that of others. . . . Seeing with their own eyes what these other people have, thrusts it within reach of their imagination and their growing capacity for resentment and envy.[3]

Countries in all parts of the Far East and Latin America are already over-urbanized, or becoming so. The drift into cities and construction sites is occurring all over the world. The better situated town dwellers are upset by the squalor and brutal crime which invade their cities. Even rigorous and socially-minded local governments have found it beyond their power to provide work and decent conditions for the thousands who want to stay near the bright lights. Officials, local and national, intone the same worry about the problem, for example, as did Sid Sampaio, Governor of

3. David Lilienthal, "Foreign Aid for the Teeming City." *The New York Times Sunday Magazine,* September 9, 1962.

the State of Pernambuco in northern Brazil: "Such populations, without means, with nothing to lose, and nothing to hope for, are fertile material for any plan or idea that seems to point the way to a better life."

They may not have the patience and submissiveness of those farm laborers and their families who flocked into the factory towns of England in the early nineteenth century. The plight of these earlier refugees from the land—crowded in the dreary slums and worn out in the mills—colored the Marx-Engels estimate of the capitalist system and their forecasts of its doom. Their fiery words find fuel again in the new slums.

The only permanent cure for such situations is to so hasten the upward swing of industry that all who seek work can find it. But in most of the poorer countries, even though generously helped, that cannot and will not happen fast enough. One reason why is because resources needed for enlarging productive activity have to be devoted to the care and support of those who have thronged into these industrial and commercial centers—to warding off epidemics, criminal assaults, riots and rebellions.

The several charges that may be imposed on the resources and judgment of local authorities and foreign aid allocators are dismaying. For they must try, at one and the same time, to expand industry which will provide useful employment for those already in the over-crowded centers and to ameliorate conditions, as well as stem or slow the exodus from the land. Confronted by these several mandates, even those officials who start as fervent believers in letting private initiative have full sway find they must resort to rigorous planning measures and impose controls and regulations. This is happening in the great municipalities of the United States.

Economic growth may also be retarded by extreme inequalities and social injustices. If these persist, industrialization is likely to lag and be interrupted by popular discontent. When ownership of property, especially of land, is markedly unequal and the division of income is grossly contorted, where small self-centered groups tax the poorer businessmen and workers while sparing themselves, and control the banks and credit, then there will be a premium on getting in with the dominant set rather than on making one's way by independent effort. The more energetic and bolder men will not seek careers in industry or commerce but in politics, the law, or the military services, or in the circle of jobbers and intermediaries. Others will decide, either because of just anger or frustration, to try to reach the top by the path of revolution.

For this reason as well as others, the American government should grasp every sensible chance to back up local persons and parties who are striving to suffuse national life with ideals and practices of social justice and open opportunity for all. Our example will count as much as our counsel and our money, and perhaps more.

Those persons in the poorer countries who assume leadership in reform programs needed for economic growth will be opposed, even reviled, by some elements in their community. Their proposals will be perverted by foes. They will suffer setbacks and defeats. Elected officials have to reckon with the risk that they may be ejected from office by those afraid of being hurt by reform. Or if the projected reform has popular appeal, political rivals, in and out of the government, may oppose it because they do not wish its sponsors to win the credit and praise.

The most outspoken and powerful opponents of reform are usually the wealthier and privileged few. They convince themselves, their dependents and followers that almost any action advocated to correct inequalities and protect the poorer and weak working millions will open the door to Communism. But in some countries, proposed moderate reforms may also be fought stubbornly by trade unions. The leaders of those that are Communistic or strongly anti-capitalist, bent either on winning mass support or bringing about economic collapse, may hinder reforms by excessive demands for wages and social welfare legislation. The leaders of more conservative trade unions may oppose them in order to preserve some questionable concession won in the past—as, for example, a four- or five-hour day in government offices, or the assignment of more workers than are needed to operate a train, unload a ship, staff a hotel. Resistance to change is to be expected where work is hard to get and desperation and hunger hound those who are without it. Even where this is not so, as in the United States, "featherbedding" is not unknown, nor collusion between monopolies and unions.

Most connected programs of foreign economic aid and domestic reform have been aligned to proceed along "the middle way." Their executors often have to proceed toward their objectives between ranks of opponents on the far right and left. When these two join to belabor a moderate reform program, then sometimes the only group that can prevent disorder and stagnation centers in or around the local military organization. The American choice is then to suspend our aid and let events take their course, or to work with the group which has taken over power, in the hope that by helping the country to better its economic condition the way will be re-opened for a return to a democratically controlled and stable regime.

Foreign-aid representatives and technicians in the poorer countries must inure themselves not only to such vicissitudes but also to the everyday trials which may interfere with their efforts to improve the material condition of the poorer peoples in whose midst they work.[4]

Those who must be taught may not know the language of the foreign tutor and he may not know theirs. The learners may be inept or overconfident. They may be unwilling to leave the towns and campuses and live in the country and the villages where the work has to be done. They may think it beneath them to work with their hands and associate with men and women who work with their hands. Their real interest may be in politics rather

4. On this point my thoughts were stimulated by an unpublished article written by Lewis Smith, a staff member of the Puerto Rican Development Authority.

than in the trade or profession they are learning. Or their real purpose in studying may be to qualify for better positions in another country.

The visiting helper can contend against such problems hopefully if he knows that the local government cares deeply about the work in which he is engaged. But if it does not, his efforts to overcome them may be doomed to failure and his period of service may end in disappointment.

The best of programs, the most able and devoted of technicians can be defeated by bad local political practices or adverse political occurrences. How can the professional career service needed to carry a country forward be developed if those who select the persons to be trained cling to the spoils system, or put personal loyalty or family connection above merit? What can foreign advisers achieve if a jealous cabinet officer prevents acceptance of their proposals because they would increase the influence of a rival colleague? Or if some civilian or military branch of the government opposes their advice, its share of government expenditures may be adversely affected. How can foreign technicians carry out well projects which take time if the officials on whom they must rely for support are often changed, or if the trained native associates on whom they depend are caught in a whirl of frequent political turnover? In short, the foreign helpers are always exposed to the hazards of local political circumstance as well as to the darts of critics and opponents.

Like public officials and reformers in all countries, rich and poor, they will come up against resistance due to avarice or rascality. Measures they propose or the administrative procedures they recommend may endanger the fortunes of those who are thriving on unjust, illegal or dishonest practice. One of their proposals might lessen the chance to escape taxation. Another might lessen the chance to smuggle goods into the country. Another might compel landlords to lower rents on slum properties. Another might make it harder for insiders to obtain government contracts by bribery. Another might interfere with the profitable practice of some lawyers defending illicit real-estate transactions. Another might arouse the wrath of squatters in the rural regions, and of cattle rustlers and bandits, by urging more drastic police action. In short, the band of foreign technicians always has to fight the devil in man and society; and he is to be praised if he does much more than hold his own.

During the past two years a novel attempt has been made to make the associations between American instructors and the foreigners they help more equal and intimate. The American government has formed a Peace Corps, assigned to whatever places and jobs for which foreign authorities request their help. This is a new form of foreign service—more akin to missionary work than to ordinary official activity. The men and women sent out on assignment are mostly young, and each of them is presumably trained in some specialty and qualified to instruct in it. Most of its several thousands of members are stationed in rather remote towns or villages and live among those whose hard and poor lives they are sent to improve. In a score of countries they are teaching in the schools, working or giving instruction on the farms, helping to build health centers and other housing, surveying roads and giving advice about the operation, maintenance and repair of tools and machines. They live and move among the natives without diplomatic caché or formality.

But neither the burrs of politics nor the ruses of rascality may be as troublesome as the resistance of those who fear or dislike the social changes which the foreign presence and proposals may bring about. The relations between the sexes, between parents and children, masters and servants, priests and parishioners, town and country may—will—be disturbed if the recommended new ways of working are adopted, and novel activities are begun. The crust of custom can be thick and resistant even when there is a great longing for a less toilsome and healthier life.

9 | Still Other Hindrances

While trials of nature may be dealt with forthrightly, hindrances to economic growth due to human traits or ways often cannot be. They may therefore be the more baffling. Records abound of the troublesome forms of conduct and custom encountered in poor countries by planners, teachers, missionaries, engineers and economists. Their renditions of their experiences, some cheerful, some woeful, are reminders of the diversity of conceptions of life and death, of love, marriage, family, public authority, duty, and war. Together they form a catalogue of the kinds of behavior that have kept peoples poor and miserable.

In some societies, men think it beneath their dignity to do hard, dirty, dreary work, outdoors and indoors, which women or children can do. There are burdensome family obligations, tribal rules and loyalties, religious taboos which stand in the way of individual initiative and advancement. There are observances harmful to health, mind or spirit. There are circumambient mistrusts and envies which hinder group effort and organization. There are the lusts for excitement and killing which spread ruin.

Any or many or all of these baneful ways impede strivings which could carry the community forward. Those individuals who might lead the way find their efforts thwarted by the astute schemers who rule many poor societies—tribal heads, spoiled monarchs, brutal military commanders, medicine men, voracious religious orders, tax collectors, land proprietors and usurers, who together manage to exact any small surplus that might have been saved.

In trying to persuade a community to correct its ways, to drop injurious customs and amend obstructive laws, the diplomat of economic development must be both zealous and prudent. He must be sure that the changes he advocates will be helpful and not too disruptive. Rarely able to impose rules of good conduct, to get them adopted he must rely mainly on the proof of the benefits that aid may bring.

When pleas and reasoning fail, he may sometimes find that his own brand of guile and appeals to vanity and selfish interest, or to the wilder streaks of human nature, may succeed in opening a way to growth. Innovators in the more primitive lands or among peoples bound by rigid custom can tell tales like that of the English engineer, Bailey, in charge of the construction of a railway through the Khyber Pass. When all other overtures to the chief of the Zakka Khel tribe through whose territory the railroad was to run were met with the answer, "Forbidden, Forbidden," Bailey tried another tack: Do you understand, he asked, that "a train through these hills could not dash to and fro at high speed. It must crawl up steep gradients. It would be laden with rich merchandise . . ." The chief stared, half-incredulous, then shouted with laughter and translated the joke to his fellows; "The Sahib builds the railways. We loot the trains." [1]

In short, the conductors of economic aid may sometimes have to stoop to befriend.

Every country is justified in protecting itself against foreign domination or exploitation. But when one that greatly needs foreign investments, loans and grants refuses, because of unjustified fear or national pride, to accord foreign purveyors reasonable

1. *The Unsung: A Record of the British Service in India,* London, 1945, pages 128–129.

satisfaction, it harms itself. Foreign suppliers—public and private—of the means for material improvement can properly be required to conform to the social ideas of the host country—save those that are very obstructive and baneful. They should be mindful of the wish of every country to control its own affairs. But they must not be faced with barriers which condemn their efforts to failure or subjected to impositions that are plainly malevolent.

Excessive nationalism will have all the more harmful effect upon those countries which by historical chance are only small fragments of territory, scattered about the globe like large rock boulders deposited by glacial advances or recessions. Nearly two score of such countries exist, dispersed on every continent; the small island states in the Caribbean and in Central America; the pinched-in little states of Southeast Asia, the sprawling aggregation of former English, French and Italian colonies in Africa, the smaller Arab components of the former Ottoman Empire—the sheikdoms along the Persian Gulf, and Jordan and Syria—the separated island fragments such as Cyprus, Zanzibar and Malagasy. More are still emerging from the rough surf of change which separates them from former masters and mentors. Most are inward-looking in their politics and plans, each expressing its wish to be treated as an equal by equipping itself with all the outward and wasteful paraphernalia of nationalism, costly public buildings, diplomatic missions, armed forces, air lines.

A very few of the small and strutting national states can prosper since they contain some vastly rich and exportable resource such as oil. The rest, if adequately helped, may be able to move ahead a little; to build roads, improve sanitation, increase water supply, and make better use of their land and take better care of their livestock, turn out more in small workshops. But they cannot go far forward, since they will be unable to provide themselves with modern productive equipment needed to overcome the more serious obstacles of nature, to expand and diversify exports and sustain modern factories. In those whose climate is benign the people may be contented if they learn to ward off and to heal sickness and have enough food and protective shelter. Or their first national effort may give way to lethargy, and their people may be responsive to demagogic leaders who mislead and misrule them, so that they continue to scrabble to keep alive.

For most of these diminutive countries the better chance of economic progress is by integrating, commercially and politically, with or into larger units. Several movements of the sort are under way. A dynamic start, in its first phase economic, has been made by five Central American countries—Costa Rica, Nicaragua, El Salvador, Guatemala and Honduras. They have entered into a treaty for the formation of a free trade area among themselves and a common tariff by 1966. They are establishing regional institutions—financial, trade and educational. Some of the small former French colonies in Africa are being kept in step by French aid and guidance, and may be held together by association with France in the Common Market. The impulses toward union and division among the Arab states of the Middle East have been erratic but some of the large and small may sometime come together in a lasting federation—not inspired primarily by common fear and hatred of Israel. Some of the former small British colonies and protectorates have wisely chosen to stay within the economic shelter of the Commonwealth. The attempt to reunite several former British colonies in Southeast Asia has been consummated in the Malayan Federation.

Those whom history—in its insensate fury—has cast asunder are not easily brought together by reason, or by promises of aid, or by prospects of more progress in union. Local sovereignty, local political offices, local prides and rivalries stand in the way of voluntary association. In time these must yield. As contributors of aid the American government should do its best to hurry the process; and sometimes even take a calm attitude toward revolutions or local aggressions which may bring this about.

I have left to the last the greatest drag on the efforts of some of the poorest peoples to lift themselves out of poverty—overpopulation. Human fecundity is not regulated by the plight of the parents or the state of a country. Numbers may leap upward even though conditions remain stationary or lean downward. The present annual cumulative rate of population growth in the poverty-stricken countries ranges between 2.0 and 3.5 per cent. It is not easy for a country, even if generously helped from outside, to increase its rate of production much faster than that.

Most poor countries are already amply populated relative to their physical environment and some are overpopulated. Only a few have potentially great and rich natural resources. Fewer still will attract trained immigrants from industrialized countries or large infusions of private foreign capital until they prove that their will to progress is stronger than the obstacles.

A rapid increase in the numbers of their people will hurt their prospects. The chief, if not the only consequence of the application of more efficient ways of production and greater amounts of capital may be still further crowding. This seems to have been the first main effect of the great industrial revolution in England and elsewhere in Europe in the last half of the eighteenth and first half of the nineteenth centuries. As Garet Garrett once remarked, the historian can think of the chimneys of the factories reared at the time as the greatest phallic symbols ever known.

Of the several reasons why rapid increase in population makes the upward climb harder, Malthus' grim reasoning must still be borne in mind, though it has lost its imperative force. The supply of means of subsistence, especially food, may not keep pace with enlarging requirements. Since the more fertile or accessible land on which food is raised is limited, as their numbers grow, a people may have to turn to poorer or more distant ones on which they must expend more capital and labor and time to get the same amount of produce. This is the law of "diminishing returns" which haunted the classical theories of economics. And as home supplies are outrun by numbers, and a poor country becomes more dependent on foreign imports of such essentials as food and fuel, its terms of trade with the outside world are likely to worsen. For to acquire the needed means of payment, it has to force more of what it has to sell into foreign markets that are already amply supplied. In that case, it will have to work the harder even to maintain a meager level of subsistence.

In our times both of these tendencies can be offset. Improved technics, better tools, and superior uses of the land and natural resources, will enable any country to support growing numbers. But if the rate of increase in population is high and cumulative these means will not suffice. Greater and greater amounts of capital will be required, not only to increase the supply of foodstuffs but also to provide elementary necessities of life for the greater numbers who will crowd into urban slums.[2]

Even if the capital used in production is increased in the necessary proportion, there may be other causes of lag on material improvement during a period of rapid growth in numbers of the living. While the length of the useful working life is prolonged, so also is the period of child-bearing and of life expectancy. Thus it is probable that during the first two decades or so of increase, the fraction of the population steadily at work will shrink. The fraction of those who are too young or too old to labor will rise. Fewer mothers and older daughters will be free to work in field or factory if there are very young children in the family requiring their care and attention. In sum, the workers will have to share among more dependents the food, clothing, shelter and schooling that their scanty earnings provide.

To repeat, all countries can now support many more people at near a subsistence level than they could have, say, a half century ago; and they should be able to support many more twenty years

2. If the approximate estimate which has won the respect of economists and national planners is correct, for every increase in the labor force of 1 per cent an additional capital investment equal to 4 per cent of the national income may be needed to provide employment on existing terms, for the increasing numbers. See Colin Clark's interesting article, "Population Growth and Living Standards" in the *International Labour Review*, August 1953.

from now. But the rate of improvement of most presently poor countries will be retarded by exceedingly rapid growth in population. The effect and abilities needed to achieve and retain any improvement at all will be harder. Much of the needed supply of capital, both domestic and foreign, will be exhausted in order merely to sustain the increasing numbers; incomes will remain small, and unemployment will remain large. Then look for more intense social strains and livelier discontents.

The chances of taking care of a rapidly increasing population are, of course, worsened if the wealthier people in the country send and keep much of their liquid capital abroad. There has been a pronounced exodus of domestically-owned capital from countries in Latin America, the Middle East and Southeastern Asia, which cannot spare it. The owners have not been disposed to invest their savings in productive enterprise at home. Some of it is put in real estate, supplemented by bank loans, to be repaid as inflation lessens the value of the currency. Some is hoarded by purchasing gold, precious jewels and famous paintings. But great amounts are banked abroad or used to buy foreign securities.

The flight of private domestic capital has many adverse consequences. It depletes the economy, augments the need for foreign aid and stimulates recourse to state initiative and ownership. It leaves poor countries without those trained native business executives, accountants, engineers, chemists and other skilled personnel who would have grown up with expanding capital investment.

Some capital takes flight to evade even moderate tax impositions, and some to escape the impact of rapid inflation.[3] But the main cause has been fear of seizure, insurrection, revolution and

3. Inflation, resulting from deficit financing, may often be useful—and sometimes essential—in accelerating or sustaining economic growth in poorer countries. But, if rapid, it is very likely to stimulate the flight of capital abroad. Another adverse consequence: the wage-earners, small merchants, sellers of services and pensioners may be injured rather than helped if this is the chief means of financing growth.

civil war. Who, in some of these countries, can foretell when he may find it prudent to follow his capital or to go into forced exile? Here is another circle of cause and effect.

The flight of capital increases the risks to which the capital that remains is subject, since it makes harder the task of lessening distress and discontent. Regrettably, planned efforts at relief may accelerate the outflow of capital during an interim period. For they usually bring increased taxation of large incomes, more stringent tax collection, redistribution of land ownership, and social welfare legislation.

There are no quick and sure ways of ending the outward movement of private capital from countries that need it. It can be hindered by exchange controls, by requiring nationals to sell foreign currency and assets to a government fiscal agency, and by subjecting the purchase of foreign assets to license. Some possessors of capital may be frightened into retaining it at home by severe penalties or threats of seizure. However, many of those who want to get it out of the country are adept in evading such controls and penalties. They are skilled in concealment and aided by banking anonymity. The only really effective way to keep domestic capital at work within the country is to offer the lure of good prospects of gain and a feeling of security. Foreign aid may play a crucial part in fostering the requisite environment.

The summary import of this review of the obstacles that lurk in the path of economic growth is this: that in order to derive much benefit from the available foreign help, the people of the poor countries must display a higher grade of personal and political conduct than must those of the more prosperous ones. They must do so to break out of the circle of poverty once and for all.

Our duty and desire are to help them. But when and despite our efforts to do so, any fail and fall back, it will be healthier for them as well as for us to locate the blame where it belongs, and not, as we have been inclined to do, take it upon ourselves. The American people may be reproached and criticized—as they are in various passages in this essay—for not giving other countries enough assistance, soon enough and steadily enough. But they must not come to regard it as axiomatic that they are to blame if the hindrances are not overcome, and castigate themselves for the faults and deficiencies of others. Candor in judgment of others —as well as in self-judgment—will be, on the whole, healthier than undue anxiety about hurting the susceptibilities of those foreign countries who will not do what they must do, and what they alone can do, to clear their own path to improvement of the material conditions of their life.

Part three |

WHAT TO ASK OF
RECIPIENTS OF AID

10 | What to Ask of Recipients of Aid

The American government would be derelict if, while trying to be sure that our aid was of genuine benefit to recipients, it did not also use it to support and supplement our diplomacy, interests and ideals. These are the chief cognate purposes that determine what the American people are inclined to expect and ask of countries that want American governmental loans and grants. Only such stipulations as are essential to fulfill them should be imposed.[1]

But suppliers and solicitors often have divergent views of what, if any, obligation attaches to aid bestowed. The supplier may be convinced that what it asks is just and of mutual advantage. The solicitor may feel that what it is being urged to do or promise is

1.   The first systematic attempt, with which I am acquainted, to enumerate the "criteria [to] be adopted for determining which nations needing and requesting economic assistance from the United States should receive such assistance" is made in the *Report of a Study of U.S. Foreign Aid in the Middle Eastern and African Countries,* submitted by Senator Gruening to the U.S. Senate Committee on Government Operations, 88th Congress, 1st Session. October 1, 1963. Each and every one of the ten criteria has reason behind them, but together they are so strict and exigent that few if any of the presently poor countries could qualify for aid under them—and for that matter not many of the more affluent ones.

against its wish and interest, or beyond its ability. How natural for the first to believe that a poor people wanting help should prove that it is deserving and friendly! How natural for the needy country to be reluctant to give up the chance to be feckless and free to change its mind! How often may it contend that it is being asked to give up its independence or dignity in return for "a pittance." When the two cannot agree, their dialogue may crackle like that of Romeo and the Apothecary in *Romeo and Juliet.*

ROMEO: Art thou so bare and full of wretchedness, and fear'st to die? Famine is in thy cheeks, need and oppression starveth in thine eyes, contempt and beggary hang upon thy back; the world is not thy friend nor the world's law. The world affords no law to make thee rich; then be not poor, but break it and take this.

APOTHECARY: My poverty, but not my will, consents.

ROMEO: I pay thy poverty, and not thy will.

But today most weak and poor nations are proudly independent and haughty. The stronger and wealthier ones seldom care or dare to compel them to obey their will. Suppliants can rarely be choosers but they can always be bargainers and critics.

The statesmanship of aid now rests primarily on coinciding interest and kinship in common causes. Thus, suppliers and solicitors must ordinarily weave their accords out of the strands of the historical, economic, and political associations in which they are enmeshed. There is no standard or accepted pattern on which these must be fashioned.

Since there are many sensitive areas in negotiation about the stipulations attached to the rendering of aid, it is hardly to be wondered that the American government has wavered and veered. Or that now and again, it has accepted frail promises in lieu of hard and fast proofs of friendship and will to perform well.

Our ruling intention has been to provide means only for programs and projects that would contribute to the permanent improvement of the condition of the people assisted. But decision sometimes has had to be lenient. Some deviations were clearly sensible in the light of the desires of the requesting government and our own interests.

Now and again the American government has been hard-pressed to indulge some wasteful or harmful wish or whim of the ruling authorities of a foreign country—to provide arms not really needed, or machines and materials for a road to a private domain, or for a pretentious public building to impress the people, or a gorgeous hotel to gratify local officials and cozen visiting foreign dignitaries, or a fleet of limousines or planes, or an air-conditioned yacht. The question of whether or not to respond to such requests —whether in effect to bestow favors in order to gratify friends or appease critics—is not novel. The tradition that foreigners ought to show their esteem for rulers by bringing presents of more value to them than to the populace still lingers in some parts of the world. The American government has been more reluctant than European governments to make personal gifts, subsidies, and bribes to impress and suborn foreign sovereigns or officials. But the unscrupulous ways of Communism have been causing it to subdue its distaste for such means of diplomacy, and to use them when the advantage of doing so is plain and the cost small.

Harder to handle have been requests for aid recommended by their prospective popular appeal rather than by their intrinsic economic merit. On this ground also the American government has been receptive to the requests of various small towns and cities in Africa for spacious firehouses and modern motorized fire-fighting equipment. Perhaps it is also why the American government has been less exigent than it might have been in requiring proof of the economic and social soundness of requests for the means of constructing iron and steel plants in some Latin American countries; and why, particularly, it has been accommodating in providing new-style uniforms for policemen and soldiers in some countries, and more modern or expensive weapons than were needed or could be well-used in others.

I cannot refrain from giving an extreme instance of the way

in which ordinary self-interested persons may depreciate aid given for basic economic purposes and prefer expenditure on which they can see they derive an immediate pecuniary benefit.

Not long ago when I was in Madras, India, I secured the required special liquor permit granted to foreigners for the purchase of liquor. With this in hand I found my way into the small room off the lobby of the Connemara Hotel where recreants like myself were served. I told the stalwart bartender that I would like to buy a bottle of Scotch whisky. The quoted price was about $15.00. I told him that rather than be that extravagant I would drink beer. While doing so and munching potato chips, I asked him: "Does anybody buy Scotch Whisky at this price?"

B A R T E N D E R , looking at me severely, as did his assistant who wore a handsome green turban—the better to keep his books: "Yes, they even buy it when it costs $20.00."

I : "Who buys it? Americans?"

B A R T E N D E R , sneeringly: "No, not Americans," and disdainfully, "They spend nothing."

I : "Well, who does buy it?"

B A R T E N D E R : "Rich Indians, British, and most of all, the Germans." And, repetitiously, "The Americans do not spend money."

I : "They may not be free spenders in this bar, but the Americans are giving or lending millions, even billions, to India."

B A R T E N D E R : "Oh, loans."

I , emphatically: "Partly as loans, partly as gifts."

B A R T E N D E R , with a snort: "To the Indian government."

I : "For the Indian people."

B A R T E N D E R , intently scrutinizing my liquor permit and $2.00 payment I was making for a bottle of Lucky Strike Beer: "The Americans do not spend money."

But all in all, the American government has refused to countenance and finance the more slack or wayward proposals. Its standards—expressed as requirements—have been, by and large, as high or higher than political and personal relations with the petitioning authorities have permitted. The percentage of our outlay for foreign aid misspent in disregard of professional judgment, merely to appease popular desire, has been small, far smaller than that wasted because of ignorance or bad judgment, or dishonesty.

It would be foolish to censure all practices in the art of pleasing and to refrain from their use when a clear benefit may be obtained or a definite injury averted. However, the American government should continue to deplore even the occasional necessity. For aid, given and taken for projects that do not bring primary and lasting benefits, may have a degrading effect upon both supplier and recipient, and cause a mutual loss of respect. Once the practice is begun, it is hard to control or end. At home unjustified expenditures may be cited to discredit the whole American foreign aid program. Abroad they may be cited as signs that the United States is either frightened or crafty rather than seriously constructive. Such charges are harder to counter because American officials and diplomats who sponsor the deviations from the rule of merit cannot openly explain their reasons.

The same rule should also determine the division, among the many sectors of national life in each of the recipient countries, of the funds and services made available. The *total* allocated for the many applicants has usually been less than is needed even for the important beginnings that should be made. There is an inescapable problem of deciding, in regard to each applicant, how much should be provided for public works, industry, agriculture, mining, fishing, housing, health, social services and education.

The choices are tough. Ideas and ideals differ on the type of society to be nurtured. Pertinent, even essential, information is often lacking. Benefits and incidental effects are hard to determine in advance. Even the most conscientious aid officials must expect that their allocations will be criticized.

It is not enough to reckon the prospective effect of alternative uses upon the gross national product, either as valued in money or measured by an index of physical output. The impact on the distribution of income, the volume of employment, and the social and political structure and institutions must also be weighed.

Therefore, when deciding how best to use available capital or technical aid, planners and budgeteers should ask not only one set of questions—what division will most increase the gross national product—but many others. What groups, classes and regions within this or that recipient country will benefit, which will suffer? Who will bear the expense? Will employed men and women be thrown out of their jobs? Will some who are without work be able to get work at once or later on? Will the young grow up healthier, more educated, more industrious than their elders? Will the countryside be deserted as farm laborers crowd into towns and cities that have no need nor place for them? In the application of the answers to these questions, planners will often run into conflicts between the aims of productivity, humanity, and international politics.

The American government has usually relied on the readiness of solicitors of aid to justify their requests by expositions of how it will be used and why the benefit visualized is reasonably assured. When these are not convincing, the responsible American officials have pointed out that if our aid is squandered and the results are scant, criticism might compel the American government to end it. Sometimes such admonitions have stirred the foreign authorities addressed to follow a sounder course and to correct disabling faults. But sometimes they have not been effective. Then it has been clear that unless our attitude was sterner, American aid would serve only as temporary relief; the trudge out of poverty would not really begin.

Consequently, in and out of Congress the judgment has formed that all applicants for aid should be urged to formulate, alone or in consultation with American authorities and/or multinational agencies, a national plan—of some sort—for economic growth toward which the United States might contribute.

This was recommended as helpful—or perhaps essential—to the effective use of local resources and foreign help in combination. That has been the main and direct reason for fostering the practice of planning. But it was not the only one. It was one way of inducing applications for aid to qualify themselves by evidencing in their plans an earnest will to help themselves. They would be committed to make a sustained effort, to earn our expenditures by their exertion.

Moreover, the strains on diplomacy might be eased by this procedure. Foreign governments might be spared the humiliation of asking for American aid and being publicly refused. The American government might be shielded against reproaches for attaching compulsory conditions, since it could prove to the recipients that the reason for doing so was to make sure that its help would bring about their economic and social resuscitation.

For this, the American government has come to place more and more stress on the stipulation that applicants for aid should demonstrate both in planning and practice a firm will to help themselves. The imperative reasons for applying this test were clearly stated by Dean Rusk in a presentation to the Senate Committee on Foreign Relations in behalf of the Foreign Assistance Act of 1962:

> First, the fundamental and indispensable requirement for the development of a nation is the determination of its own government and people to move forward. Our aid, no matter what its amount, cannot materially help those who will not help themselves. No country can make solid progress except by its own efforts, inspired by its own leadership and supported by the dedication of its own people.
>
> The aid we can supply will be only a small portion of the total national effort needed. Our aid, for example, to the nations joining in the Alliance for Progress is less than 2 per cent of the total of their gross national product. Obviously, therefore, what is done by these nations with their own resources is crucial. But if our aid can stimulate, galvanize the 98 per cent of which I spoke, then it will have performed a very great service.
>
> But their efforts must in all cases include mobilization of national resources—economic, financial, and human. With national variations, they must include the willingness to undertake reforms important to progress—reforms in taxation, in landholdings, in housing, and the broadening and improvement of educational

opportunities. We must constantly bear in mind that our goal is not just economic development. It is equally and concurrently to increase social justice which will secure the benefits of progress to those masses who have so long suffered from poverty, ignorance, and disease—and from the most cruel condition of all, hopelessness.[2]

In accordance with these ideas, the American government has been trying to jostle all recipients of aid to plan to make the basic effort to help themselves. Theirs—we would have it—is to be the part of doers; ours the part of eager instructor and contributor of essential, but still only supplementary, means.

It is in Latin America at the present time that the American government is trying hardest to construct programs on this scaffold of conceptions, through the cooperative program brightly named the Alliance for Progress. Although the main rules which it expects active participants to observe have been repetitiously featured in official and unofficial statements, extracts from two of the more succinct may give precision to my comments.

In proposing the Alliance, President Kennedy, on March 13, 1961, explained that the allocation and disbursement of the contributed funds for the ten year program were to be conditioned on the willingness of each recipient nation to improve its own institutions, make necessary modifications in its social patterns, and mobilize its own domestic resources in a program of development. "Let me stress," he said, "that only the determined efforts of the American nations themselves can bring success to this effort. They, and they alone, can mobilize resources of a scope and magnitude sufficient to make this bold development program a success—and modify their social patterns so that all, and not just a privileged few share in the fruits of growth. If this effort is made, then outside assistance will give a vital impetus to progress—without it no amount of help will advance the welfare of the people."

The Declaration of Punta del Este adopted by the Latin Ameri-

2. Hearings, April 5, 1962.

can Republics in August 1961 signaled acceptance of the view that each and all must earn their right to receive external aid. They vowed that they would, as they could, strive to

bring about a steady and substantial improvement in the condition of their peoples by
1) Providing decent homes in city and country
2) Transforming unjust structures and systems of land tenure, and creating an equitable system of property under which owners and workers could enjoy adequate and timely credit and technical assistance
3) Wiping out illiteracy, and extending secondary and technical training
4) Pressing forward with programs of health and sanitation
5) Assuring workers fair wages and satisfactory working conditions
6) Reforming tax laws, obtaining more from those that have most; redistributing national income to benefit the needy, while also promoting savings and investment
7) Avoiding monetary inflation and deflation
8) Stimulating private enterprise and industry [3]

During their days and nights around the conference table, the representatives of the American nations were elevated into the euphoric mood where men seem perfectible; and into that dreamier one where even national states can become so. Delegates emerge from such convocations as elated and resolved as erring youths on New Year's morning. Then they go back home to mingle with the men and women who have not been uplifted and to face the realities of national faults and divisions, and the opposition of those who fear to lose income, property or status.

At Punta del Este the American government strove to strengthen the cords—and chords—of mutual obligation by proposing that each participant submit its plan of national develop-

3. This is a summary paraphrase of the professions contained in the Declaration of Punta del Este, a summary of the Charter of the Alliance for Progress.

ment and reform to a small committee—seven out of the nine Latin Americans—selected by the Organization of American States. This panel was to have scrutinized the plans submitted and solicited attention for its comments. However, the bigger and more industrialized Latin American republics—Argentina, Brazil and Mexico—were unwilling at that time to subject their national programs to this possibly unreliable or upsetting examination. The touchy task of estimating whether the self-help measures which each prospective recipient is going to take are coherent and adequate enough to warrant aid was consigned to the American government.

However, stimulated by repeated failures of most of its members to manage their affairs so that the aid given them produced the desired result, a renewed attempt was made in November 1963 to entrust a small committee with substantial authority to determine standards of merit—self-help and reform—to be applied when passing on requests for aid under the aegis of the Alliance for Progress. But again, some of the larger members—particularly Brazil—refused to subject their actions, policies and plans to collective scrutiny. The refusal was garbed in the well-worn cloak of national pride. The opponents of this proposal urged an alternative which would allow them to be more, not less lax.

The actions of many of the countries who joined in the Declaration of Punta del Este have not matched their avowals. Several, among them Brazil, Argentina, Chile and Peru, remain in economic confusion and/or political turmoil. Their precarious regimes have not been able to carry through national programs of the kind envisaged at Punta del Este. Up to now the American government has not insisted on vigorous observance of their vows; in the well-worn metaphor, it has not "pulled the reins" on its aid tautly. However, American criticism of the Alliance is becoming sharp and American willingness to provide funds for its members is being tempered by a determination to ask of each conclusive proof of their will and intention to live up to the terms of the Alliance. As I write (in November 1963) the future of this collective program is in hazard.

Not only in this hemisphere but elsewhere it has proven far from easy to adhere strictly to the policy of requiring aid-seeking governments to create a good prospect of self-help. The American government has urged all countries seeking aid to work out qualifying programs for themselves, knowing, as they would, that it was looking over their shoulder. But it has had to be careful not to lend credence to accusations that the United States was trying to dictate or dominate their national life. It has had to decide in each case whether rigid insistence that plans for self-help attain the qualifying mark was advisable; whether sternness and suspension of aid would bring about quick compliance or would merely foreclose the chance of bringing the laggard nearer the mark as the aid program proceeded.

Sometimes kindliness rather than duress has seemed more likely to induce the desired response. And sometimes severity was ruled out for reasons of foreign policy.

As ruefully admitted by Secretary of State Rusk in one of his appearances before Congress, "So we have to work with the governments that do not live up to the demands of the task, sweat with them, to try to achieve performance on their side which will make our aid effective."

The American government is now trying to coax a score of governments in all regions of the world to do what they ought to do for the sake of their people. It is accepting excuses for previous delays, and fresh promises that this time, the next time, the recipients will take the steps essential to assure that our aid stimulates a diffused growth. So, in continuing dialogue, it is striving to keep in touch with the faltering authorities of Brazil, Argentina, Chile, Peru, Bolivia, Iran, Ethiopia, Algeria, Morocco, South Korea, Laos, Vietnam, Pakistan and other countries. Time alone will tell in which cases this plodding and lenient diplomacy will be effective, and gradual economic and social progress made, and in which cases the supported governments will continue to be unable to haul their masses out of the slough of poverty.

Always somewhere, and usually in several places at once, American regulators of aid have even felt compelled for one reason or another—usually military—to give much aid—in proportion to the numbers of their nationals—to governments known to be shirking, corrupt or oppressive. How long, for example, did it down its disapproval and distrust for the Rhee regime in South Korea and the Diem-Nhu regime in Vietnam and continue to aid them—out of fear of giving the Communists a chance to extend their rule and domain?

This may indicate that the United States has roamed in too many directions in quest of political and military alliances. The basic question is whether in our relations with *all* the countries whose friendship or neutrality the American government has been trying to assure, vital American national interests are truly at stake. Given the anxious assumptions which have governed American foreign policy during the past decade, the concessions to the faults of others were prescribed. But my impression, looking back over the record, is that the American government has been too swayed by anxiety in its treatment of some of the less worthy governments that have sought its economic aid.

Influential groups and members of Congress have persistently urged that the American government should stipulate that those who want its help give wide leeway to private capital, domestic and foreign. Some would have it cease all aid to countries that do not do so. Others, more moderate, would only have it abstain from providing means to enable foreign governments to carry out projects in which private capital would engage if offered sufficient inducement or guarantees against loss.

Some of the sponsors of these proposals have been influenced by the wish to lessen public expenditure; others by the belief that private capital and industry were being deprived of the chances to profit; and still others by the conviction that publicly owned and managed enterprise is always, or almost always, more wasteful and inefficient than private. But even detached and un-dogmatic observers have gradually begun to perceive that unless directed with contrary intent, programs of public assistance may foster the extension of government activity in recipient countries. The prevalent tendency of both national and multinational lend-ing or granting institutions has been to deal with governments and conclude their transactions with them. The availability of foreign government loans and grants has often made it easier for the as-sisted authorities to engage in economic developments on better financial terms than private interests, domestic or foreign, could offer. Moreover, foreign government capital may tend to warp the flow and distribution of capital investment within the re-cipient countries. It may attract the available capital toward large public projects of the sort included in the conception of basic "infra-structure" of development, leaving less for private indus-tries, trade and agriculture. Moreover, because the recipient gov-ernment may absorb so much of the local capital to complement foreign funds, the private sectors of the economy may be less able to finance themselves, even while their chance to expand may be increased by the public expenditure.[4]

Any or all of these reasons, and others, have been advanced in support of the substantive recommendations made by special ad-visory groups headed by eminent industrialists appointed by the government. Two of those whose reports left an impress were the Randall Committee in 1954 and the Fairless Committee in 1957. As Walter Krause aptly observed in his book *Economic De-velopment*, "In short, the common attitude that had evolved [by that time] was a combination of 'end grant aid' and 'let private

4. The many interacting tendencies that have manifested themselves are perceptively explained in the book previously cited, *U.S. Private and Gov-ernment Investment Abroad*, edited by Raymond F. Mikesell.

foreign investment do the job.' " [5] Conformably John B. Hollister, then Director of what was then called the International Cooperation Administration (ICA) announced that

> The United States is convinced that private ownership and operation of industry and extractive enterprises contribute more effectively than public ownership and operation to the general improvement of the economy of the country through better management, research, quality control, lower prices, increased employment and capital growth.
>
> It is therefore a basic policy of the I.C.A. to employ United States assistance to aid-receiving countries in such a way as will encourage the development of the private sectors of their economies. Thus, I.C.A. will not normally be prepared to finance publicly owned industrial and extractive enterprise although it is realized there may be exceptions.[6]

But the exceptions soon multiplied and the rule was relaxed in the years that followed. For in some poverty-ridden countries the terms asked by private foreign capital were too onerous. In others the people or government were hard set in favor of public ownership of basic industries and natural resources. In others the dominant political groups were determined to keep control of certain branches of production as an adjunct to their political authority and an addition to their personal incomes. In such situations rigidity was likely to be ineffectual. Rebuffed authorities might turn to the Soviet Government for the help wanted in assembling capital and skills. Moreover, the International Bank for Reconstruction and Development and other international agencies did not draw a hard and fast line. In the broad realm of public utility industries they did not try to compel resistant governments to choose between giving up a prime project or turning it over to private capitalists on their own terms.

Flexibility fostered by expediency, the American government hoped, might in time cause countries to become more disposed to

5. Page 342.
6. Press Release No. 338, Sept. 12, 1957.

admit American private capital into their basic and extractive industries. For that might dispel their idea that American aid policies were dictated by a few selfish and ruthless capitalists. Acknowledgment that the tenets of private capitalism were not always decisive might bring others to recognize that extensive government ownership was not an essential complement of national independence and the only surety of general welfare.

In deference to these facts, the American government has become inured to assisting government-owned enterprises and semisocialist programs of development. And the Executive has repeatedly besought Congress not to constrain it from doing so. Thus, to take the most recent notable instance, President Kennedy, in May 1963, confirmed the willingness of the American government to help the government of India build another steel mill (at Bokaro) even though it would be state-owned and compete with privately owned mills. When quizzed by the press, his opinion emerged from the meshes of his reply.

> No. There's such a need for—such a need for steel—that's going to be unfilled and providing it's an efficient project, I would think that we could assist it if it meets what the economy of India requires. I must say that I don't quite get the logic of those who so vehemently oppose this very much needed project; not just take possession of a steel mill or reconstruct it, but to build one. There is an important distinction. At the same time when we lend hundreds of millions of dollars to Canada to join in the nationalization of the electric lights in Quebec. . . .
>
> Now I think that this is a steel mill which will go up. All the evidence we have says it will not go up unless the United States joins in, so I think we ought to do it. . . . Now Congress may have other views, but I think it would be a great mistake not to build it. India needs that steel.[7]

However, two months later the Foreign Aid Administrator David E. Bell was assuring the Foreign Affairs Committee of the House of Representatives that it would not take action on the

7. *The New York Times,* May 9, 1963.

project until next year and would heed its "strong views." Even this did not satisfy the opponents who wanted a stringent ban on loans to "state owned productive enterprises." The House of Representatives, objecting to the project on the ground that it would mean that American capital was being used to spread Socialism in India, forbade the Executive from proceeding with it during the current year. Therefore, Prime Minister Nehru informed the American government that it was willing, albeit with regret, to withdraw its request for American assistance on this project. President Kennedy thought it well to grasp this way out of the controversy. India may or may not be able to secure the needed aid elsewhere from public or private lenders. If it does not, the observation made by G. L. Bansal, the Secretary-General of the Federation of Indian Chambers of Commerce, that the ban could also hurt the private sector of Indian industry will be validated.[8] Indian industry needs more steel and India crucially needs the foreign exchange that would be saved by reduction of imports of steel.

The argument, often a muddled and partisan one, over this general issue, gives expression to resurgent protests both in and out of Congress against the extension of state control of economic life with American assent and assistance. These were reflected in the injunctions of the report of the Clay Committee in 1963 that the American government must try harder to get foreign governments to remove the impediments to private capital. Responsively, President Kennedy—in the message he sent to Congress about the proffered foreign aid bill for 1964—reverted to the tone and tenor of President Truman's presentation in 1949 of the Point IV program, stressing that:

> The primary new initiative in this year's program relates to our increased efforts to encourage the investment of private capital in the under-developed countries.

and he remarked also

8. *The New York Times,* Sept. 8, 1963.

I believe much more should be done, however, administratively and through more vigorous action by the Agency for International Development, and legislatively by the Congress. Administratively, our Ambassadors and missions abroad, in their negotiations with the less developed countries are being directed to urge more forcibly the importance of making full use of private resources and improving the climate for private investment, both domestic and foreign.[9]

He proposed that a special tax credit be accorded on new private investment and re-investment in developing countries, and he suggested that the insurance guarantees against loss obtainable by investments abroad be made even more comprehensive.[10] Congress, in sympathy with this purpose, greatly increased the maximum sum of the guarantees that may be issued. However, lest the issuances of these guarantees lessen the hesitation of a foreign government to dispossess a private American enterprise—the pertinent legislation stipulates that guarantees are to be issued only for investments in countries whose governments sign self-restraining accords with the American government. This, many of the aid-seeking countries have been loath to do.

One reason for the re-emphasis of need to rely upon private capital was the change in the balance of payments situation of the United States, and the large out-flow of gold. Greater reliance on private capital, it was hoped, would lessen the drain. This thought eclipsed concern over the fact that the subsequent remittances of interest or profit to private American investors would make future requisitions on the foreign exchange resources of the recipient countries greater than repayments that they would have had to make on an equivalent amount of government loans or

9. Message, President Kennedy to Congress on the Foreign Aid Program, April 2, 1963.

10. Under existing legislation the President may, on payment of fees, issue guarantees against losses incurred because of currency inconvertibility, expropriation or confiscation, war, revolution or insurrection. It may also issue special guarantees against losses of loan investments in housing, projects furthering social progress and those directed to the development of small business enterprises.

grants. Those who directly invest their own capital in foreign countries expect a substantial rate of return that can be regularly remitted.

But because the gold losses had continued and American purchases of the stocks and bonds of foreign companies and governments (portfolio investment) have increased markedly, the American government has recently decided that they must be checked. President Kennedy proposed, and Congress has approved, the imposition of what is termed an "interest equalization" tax on future purchases of such securities from foreigners. However, since this tax does not apply to "direct" investment by American companies or groups in ventures they control, and since, in any case, Americans would not have purchased a substantial amount of the securities originating in the poorer countries, they will not be hurt. Unless exemptions are made, this tax might hinder the efforts of any that in the future should discover and want to keep in their own national control oil or abundant and salable mineral or other natural resources. More probably, however, the capital for this purpose that could not be procured by sale of securities to private American investors could be had elsewhere.

Consistently, during the past decade, the American government had until recently become less responsive to requests that it extend the mantle of official protection over the thousands of privately owned American enterprises established abroad. It has been using its diplomatic power in their behalf lightly, and its military power never.

In fact, fear of provoking reprisals against large existing American private foreign equity (for example, chemicals, oil, copper, iron ore, rubber, tin or telephones) in a foreign country have now and again caused the American government to be more forthcoming with its own funds. It has been induced to provide desired aid lest a disgruntled foreign government exact what it wanted from the American private enterprises subject to its will or nationalize them. So Nasser acted against the Suez Canal Company after the American government held back from financing the Aswan dam. So Castro acted against American private enterprises after the American government ended preferential treatment for Cuban sugar. So officials in other countries have hinted they or their successors might also have to act unless the American government helps them to allay popular discontent or buy off opposition. Thus, large American private foreign investments in politically disturbed countries may be not only a hostage to their owners but a vexation in the conduct of American government aid.

American opinion has been balking at the practice of continuing aid to foreign authorities who harden their treatment of private American investments or nationalize them without compensation. Indignation made Congress respond to the outcry that this must not be allowed to go on. In the Foreign Assistance Act of 1962 it directed the President to suspend assistance to any foreign government which expropriated, nationalized or seized control of American-owned property if that government did not give fair and prompt compensation in convertible foreign exchange.[11]

By dint of its pleas not to shackle American diplomacy, the Executive managed to persuade Congress to loosen the language of the pertinent provision, but was not given discretion to waive it.[12] The State Department pointed out that a rigid mandatory rule would place American foreign policy at the hazard, on the one hand, of a reckless or estranged foreign official who might wish to obstruct our aid program; and, on the other hand, of a selfish and shortsighted American company whose conduct might have educed the act of expropriation. Moreover, it explained that it is sometimes hard to judge the warrant which the local government may have for its act of expropriation. The American private inter-

11. Foreign Assistance Act of 1962. Amendment to Subsection (e) of Section 620 of Foreign Assistance Act of 1961.
12. An able statement on the subject was submitted by the State Department to the Committee on Foreign Relations of the Senate of the 87th Congress, Second Session, Hearings on the Foreign Assistance Act of 1962, pages 557–558.

ests concerned may decry its action as willful and unjust. But more detached minds may find it defensible. It may be incidental to a sweeping effort to lessen economic and social inequality, bearing no harder on foreigners than on nationals; as for example when large American-owned tracts of farming, grazing or timber lands are taken over for redistribution, or when American-owned slum property is condemned in order that low cost housing may be built.

How exigent should the American government be if the act is taken under pressure of driving circumstance or demanding public opinion that threatens the tenure of office of the local authorities? This question arises particularly in regard to the take-over of American-owned regulated public utility companies—local transport, light and power, telephone—caught in the spiral of inflation. Either from fear of popular protest or because of a wish to hold down the cost of living, local public authorities may refuse the companies permission to increase the rates they charge as much or as fast as would be necessary to earn a profit and enable them to expand its services out of income. However, under the stimulus of inflation and depressed rates, public demands for these services is likely to grow. So does the critical clamor, if the demands are not met. In such circumstances the local authorities may feel they have no choice but to expropriate now and perhaps pay later. This is easier for them than to allow adequate rate increases or severely to restrain inflation, since most of their constituents do not realize that in one way or another they will have to pay for the services they want.

Of course, sometimes local authorities may be glad to have a good pretext for doing what they were eager to do anyhow. For example, informed observers had the impression that Señor Miguel Arras de Alençar, Mayor of Recife, the intellectual and political center of radical opinion in Brazil, was just waiting for a good excuse to take over the local subsidiary of the American and Foreign Power Company. Ignoring the company's plea that it could not afford to do what he asked and extend street lighting to the whole of the city unless allowed to raise its rates, the Mayor expropriated the company. What, he demagogically asked, would the American government do if ". . . a Brazilian company operating in the United States had failed to provide street lights. Don't you think the people would react?" [13]

Equally hard, it should be observed, may be the settlement of what is fair compensation. Must investors be requited not only for loss of what they have invested, but also for the chance to make profits in the future?

In my judgment, the problem in the public utility field is so fraught with conflicting equities and exigencies that the American Executive authorities ought to be left free to act as they judge best in the face of each situation—to be firm or compromising or yielding.

However, since the same possibly extenuating causes are usually lacking, and since the United States has so much more at stake, the Executive should as a rule be sternly resistant to threats of expropriation made without just cause against American-owned companies in other branches of activity in which public welfare is not so widely affected. Of particular concern are those in which very large sums have been invested to develop a natural resource—especially oil and metals. They should be supported up to the limit of our diplomatic influence in their opposition to unfair demands. In the event that a foreign country proceeds in the face of our protest to dispossess such an American enterprise, the government should be prepared to deprive the offending government of aid unless it reverses its action or makes adequate compensation. Expropriation of the American-owned extractive enterprises in foreign countries will not only hurt the United States but set back the economy of the expropriators; for few, if any, would be able themselves to supply the sums needed for expansion, even if they run the nationalized enterprises on business lines. Moreover, their contribution to total world supply being dispensable, they would

13. *The New York Times*, May 19, 1962.

probably not be able to sell in the West as much of the product of the seized enterprises as had the private owners. Hence they might be tempted to enter into barter agreements with the Communist bloc.

Foreign companies in the extractive industries can sometimes do much to quench the opinion that they are exhausting local wealth without rendering sufficient return to the local community; by sharing their profits generously with the local governments, by schooling and training the natives, and by contributing to the general welfare of the country. By these means and others, the larger American companies abroad have fitted themselves into the environment of some of the countries in which they are engaged so well and have given so much satisfaction that the communities regard them with favor. But in others nothing they can do within reason has stemmed the fused assault of excited nationalism, Socialist antagonism and political envy.

The issue arose most recently and disturbingly when, in November 1963, the newly elected President of Argentina, Arturo Ilia, annulled as illegal the contracts into which his predecessors had entered with foreign oil companies—mainly American—to explore for and develop Argentine oil resources. In good faith they had invested several hundreds of millions of dollars. In an effort to avert the action, the American government hurried Under-Secretary of State Harriman down to Buenos Aires. He tried to convince Ilia that the action would hurt Argentina, since it would both discourage private foreign investment in Argentina and endanger the appropriation by Congress of that continuing assistance the American government was pledged to offer in accord with the program of the Alliance for Progress. But hardly had Harriman left when the contracts were cancelled. The President's comments on possible terms of renegotiation or compensation were murky and changeable. Appropriations for future aid for Argentina are in doubt and will certainly be made contingent on either a mutually acceptable revision of the contracts or a satisfactory and reliable offer of compensation.

Provoked by this episode, Congress inserted into the Foreign Assistance Act of 1963 a provision directing the President to suspend assistance to any government "that has taken steps to repudiate or nullify existing contracts or agreements with any United States citizen or any corporation, partnership, or association not less than 50 per centum beneficially owned by United States citizens." [14]

The advocates of a strong and firm stand hope thereby to impress upon those recipients of American aid in which American private enterprises operate that if they dispossess these enterprises or injure them unfairly they will injure their own best chances of economic growth. For in the long run they will have to look to private capital rather than to the American Treasury for the means of extending their industrial development. The Communist bloc will not come to their rescue unless its own purposes, not the recipients', are served, first and last.

American experience, thus far, has been too brief and variable to indicate whether this mode of expressing our dissatisfaction will cause willful offenders to be more considerate, or more defiant. But I believe that it will usually prove healthy in most situations.

14. Foreign Assistance Act of 1963. Section 620 (2) (e).

11 | What Else to Ask of Recipients of Aid

American effort to support fair "ground rules" for private capital is encompassed within a more inclusive stipulation—the connotation of which is still not clear.

Henceforth, President Kennedy stated in his message to Congress in March 1961,

> At the center of the new effort must be national development programs. It is essential that the developing nations set for themselves sensible targets; that these targets be based on balanced programs for their own economic, educational and social growth —programs which use their own resources to the maximum. . . . These national development programs—and the kind of assistance the free world provides—must be tailored to the recipients' current stage of development and their foreseeable potential.

Not long ago both the idea and practice of national planning were deemed unnecessary and objectionable. Unnecessary, because—so it was then thought—those who risked their own private capital and careers, if left alone, would produce the goods and services most wanted, and by investing their earnings they would propel economic life forward. Objectionable, because government planning would suppress individual initiative and put incompetent politicians in control of economic affairs.

But now the American government and international aid agencies are requesting applicants for aid to formulate plans of national effort into which their aid is to fit. They praise and promise to pamper those who make a conscientious effort to improve their planning process. As affirmed not long since by Fowler Hamilton, at the time head of the Agency for International Development (AID): "If a country's leaders appreciate and apply a national approach to resource allocation and are actively working toward a national plan, this justifies our assisting a program conditioned on progressive implementations of planning standards." [1]

The reversal of attitude began when the rapid and sustained rate of industrial advance in the Soviet Union made its impact on thought here and abroad. This routed the view that comprehensive planning under government direction must surely end in failure. During the Second World War all belligerents resorted to some measure and kind of planning, to systems of enforced priorities. The practice thus made familiar was brought out of the shadows into good repute by the success of the less rigid plans and less compulsory methods used by participants in the Marshall Plan. Their experience was taken as evidence not only of the value of some kind of planning, but also as an indication that it was compatible with the preservation of private capital and enterprise.

These opinions met less resistance as the American government learned how hard it was to make a good start on relieving poverty in backward countries. It concluded that one reason why American aid did not produce the hoped-for results was that neither the contributors nor recipients of aid were guided by an advance prospectus of the whole national effort.

Without planning, the aid administrators began to ask them-

1. See statement of Fowler Hamilton, the Administrator of AID, June 8, 1962, presented to Subcommittee of Committee on Appropriations of the House of Representatives. Hearings, vol. 2, pages 101–102. Secretary of State Rusk's statement had the same import. *Ibid.*, page 8.

selves, how can we know whether the projects financed by the American government will fit in with others under way, so that there will be a balanced reciprocal and sustaining demand for what can be produced? How else assure the proper conjunction of innovations which would conjure up those "external economies" which enable industries to become efficient and expand?

And, above all, in what other way can we make sure that recipients will devote enough of their productive effort to the creation of capital goods needed to keep them going ahead without more and more external aid? The record hinted that this would not come about in poorer countries without deliberate direction. Their peoples are so eager for any personal goods or services they can afford to buy, that of their own volition they will save little. Even should the volume of goods produced on the farms and in the factories begin to rise as a result of aid, the margin set aside as capital might not increase since the workers might demand higher wages and more expensive social services. Thus most of the poorer countries will only channel enough of their current effort into the creation of the capital needed to enlarge future production if they purposefully set out to do so.

As this reasoning left its impress, what was formerly regarded as a regrettable necessity turned into an esteemed practice. Other advantages were also discerned in this new trend of thought, professional and official. Planning—with its dramatic vista of a better life—might be a good way to enlist the support and ardor of those called on to work harder, to change their ways, to move, to assent to heavier taxation, to save and to cooperate. The planning procedures brought the Americans engaged in the administration of aid into closer association with those individuals and groups in each recipient country who are serious and single-minded in their desire for development. They might as well enable the American authorities to dispose of inferior proposals without giving offense. In these and other ways, it is conceived, planning might not only improve the results of our aid but also improve relations between those helping and those helped. Colleagues in consultation may come to think of themselves as compeers and so less mindful of any differences of nationality, color, race and status.

The American authorities have no standard model plan in mind. They know that the objectives, the dimensions, and the contents of each national plan will and should be different for each applicant; no two are ever alike. Nor are the contemplated procedures for putting the plans into effect.

The spectrum of planning and plans is very wide. Of all shades and shapes, it may be said that they are activated by the wish of their designers to know ". . . what you are doing, where you are going, and to the extent humanly possible, how you are going to get there." [2] Also, as is commonly remarked in conservative milieus such as the International Bank for Reconstruction and Development and the U.S. Treasury, "it is a way of illuminating choices." But these are only comments on the general purposes of planning. They do not dispose of the issues that present themselves in the course of planning.

Many, if not most of the national plans recently produced imply more or less definitely, as Gunnar Myrdal has pointed out, that "quite apart from the question of where the line is drawn between public and private responsibility . . . the national government is expected to assume by means of the plan, and the coordinated system of state interferences making up the operational part of it, responsibility for the direction of the entire economic development of the country." [3] And almost all of them, as he has also correctly observed, ". . . proclaim a decision to increase the total amount of investment aimed at raising the productive powers of the country and to define the means by which this can be done." [4]

Along with these rough identities there are, as has been remarked, numberless variations between plans. So many are there

2. Statement of Frank H. Coffin, Deputy Administrator of AID, Hearings on Foreign Assistance Act of 1962, Senate Committee on Foreign Relations, April 12, 1962, page 337.

3. Gunnar Myrdal, *Rich Lands and Poor,* page 82.

4. *Ibid.* page 83.

that any serious attempt to classify them would turn into a long treatise of its own.[5] Even the briefest of notes may clarify a little the vast differences in nature, scope, methods, and productive lineaments of the presentations which are all given the name of "plans."

One is the sort of plan in effect in the Soviet Union. That is based on complete state ownership of the primary means of production, including land. Workers, high and low, are servants of the state which issues orders to all and rewards and punishes. Under imposed and comprehensive plans of this kind the government determines what is to be produced, and in what amounts, and who is to get what; or it tries its utmost so to do. Prices, wages, the use of savings are fixed by authority. So are places to live and chances for an education. In short, the plan, conceptually representing the interest and striving of the whole society, is the master; all individuals are its agents.

The American government, its Western associates, and the international financial agencies they support, have eschewed this all-engrossing type of plan and the methods of compulsion by which it is enforced. For it is a demeaning kind of servitude for its subjects, and it confers a despotic and dangerous degree of power on its rulers. Moreover, in countries less spacious and well endowed by nature than the Soviet Union, and peoples harder to drill and rule, such plans would surely break down—as is partially the case in Communist China.

However, the American government has assisted in the execution of plans under which the sector of public ownership and direction is wide, embracing many basic economic activities—banking and insurance, railways, steamship and air lines, coal mines and oil refineries, gas fields and pipe lines, electric utilities, steel mills and even automobile, fertilizer and chemical plants. These

5. Seymour E. Harris included most of the main varieties in the collection edited by him entitled *Economic Planning: The Plans of the Fourteen Countries with Analyses of the Plans.* New York, 1949. The analyses bring out the essential similarities and differences. However, the plans reviewed have undergone much subsequent change.

also may set or strictly regulate the prices and marketing of farm products. Varied prototypes of plans with so considerable a component of state ownership and control are, for example, now in effect in India and some of the Latin American countries. But the American government has provided support for them where and when they were adopted by constitutional methods and were introduced by popular consent. And only where and when farmers, laborers and technicians have a genuine choice of work or occupation, and owners of private capital can keep a good portion of it and are allowed a substantial chance to use it to build businesses of their own outside of the fields foreclosed by the government.

Under such semi-socialist plans official powers are invoked in whatever ways and to whatever extent are required to carry out primary objectives. Direct commands may not be issued. But in flexible combination governments use their power to tax, to borrow, to lend, to subsidize and to requisition. They may also regulate the inauguration, location, development and financing of private enterprises. At the same time, they may confer favor on some branches of private economic activity—in agriculture, industry, construction, trade, professional and personal services; by, for example, providing at low cost, water, transport, fertilizers, tools, electric power, storage facilities and technical schooling.

But most of the plans in use or under discussion with the American government contemplate a still smaller measure of government ownership, control or regulation. The principal purposes of such plans are the same as those of more comprehensive ones; to assure that those activities which are deemed essential to material improvement will secure enough scarce capital and skills to reach the production goals in mind, and to coordinate new economic ventures. They also provided for such resort to government powers as is thought necessary to direct the elements of production into the channels of assigned priorities.

The meaning of the terms "plan" and "planning" has been stretched to include even what are in reality only official studies of national resources and projections of the ways in which they could best be used. The value of any such study depends entirely on its quality. Its effectiveness depends on the depth and correctness of its grasp of the human inclinations that rule the particular society and its political and economic divisions. Even though some of the surveys of this kind which have been produced are only summaries of the obvious, and others rather empty statistical indicators of what is theoretically possible, the American government is well advised to encourage applicants for aid to make thorough preliminary studies of their means and the requirements for material progress.

Sponsors of the practice of national planning differ in their opinions of the ways in which it will affect the prospects of private capital and enterprise in poorer and undeveloped countries. This is not to be wondered at since each commentator may have in mind a different kind of "planning."

But experience indicates that in the poorer countries, no matter what their predisposition, governments have to supply much of the impetus and capital needed to get any large innovating plan going. For up to now in these countries neither domestic nor foreign private capital will take the lead; it will wait until acceptable opportunities are created. To overcome their hesitations and fears, the American government, as has been noted, is offering tax concessions, easy government credit, and insurance against loss to private American investors in the undeveloped countries.

In actuality, local government action based on plans may in many of the more poor and stagnant countries be the necessary prelude to any substantial expansion of private economic activity. This is the thought behind the answer which W. W. Rostow gave when asked whether the planning process would not lead to subordination of both domestic and foreign private capital:

> It might seem strange that the United States so deeply attached to the virtues of private enterprise should be an advocate of national planning in the undeveloped areas. However, there was no

incompatibility. The framework within which a modern private enterprise system could develop must largely be created initially by the effort and initiative of the government.[6]

This surmise may or may not be validated by further experience. It cannot be if a plan contemplates that the government acquire for its own undertakings almost all, or all, of the accretions of capital, domestic and foreign, and technicians. Once started along that way, governments have seldom retreated; they have rarely given up economic ground that they have occupied.

While approving national planning, the American government has tried hard to see that it did not end by making the governments of recipient countries supreme arbiters of economic affairs. As already remarked, it has constantly reminded them that they will have to look to the owners of private capital for most of the foreign resources they will need; and so they had better not impair their own future by engrossing all the main fields of economic activity, and banning or unduly restricting private enterprise. This view of the desired dual function of the planning process was most recently stated by the Clay Committee, "Sound governmental planning consists of establishing intelligent priorities for the public investment program and formulating a sensible and consistent set of public policies to encourage growth in the private sector." Most American officials and private consultants who are working in, with, or for the governments of needy countries in their planning, are giving the same counsel and trying to see that it is heeded.

Planning may bring about a more sober estimation of what a nation can accomplish. Thereby it may dispel wild ideas and promises of politicians and leaders of opinion. Or it may over-excite their desires and imaginations and so cause them to set their

6. *The New York Herald Tribune,* Feb. 27, 1962.

hearts on unattainable objectives. How easy it is, for example, to be carried away by calculations of how much better off a country would be if its supply of electric power were quadrupled, especially if engineers find that it could be quadrupled were a great and tumultuous river to be channeled and dammed and a huge power plant built; and so a project is included in a plan even though the means for carrying it out are nowhere in sight—not at home, not abroad.

Thus the introduction of the practice of planning can lead to an increase in the requests and levies by the poorer countries upon all foreign sources of assistance. When political leaders find that their national plans and promises have outrun achievement, they may try to put the blame on parsimonious wealthy foreign countries. They may seek to redeem their pledges and save themselves by intimating to hesitant suppliers that unless given more help they will be compelled to turn to the other side in the cold war, or be ejected from office by other men who will not hesitate to do so. Such, for example, have been the tactics occasionally followed by Prime Minister Nehru in India, President Ayub Khan in Pakistan, President Nkrumah in Ghana, and President Goulart in Brazil.[7] The Soviet Union is as subject to this same sort of pressure from some of the countries aligned with it. It can be assumed, for example, that the Soviet authorities are approving Castro's large requisitions because he keeps warning them that unless he can make Socialism work in Cuba, sooner or later that country will return to the capitalist fold.

---

7. Countries which are not recipients of foreign government assistance may find themselves compelled to seek trade concessions from others in order to make good on objectives set forth in national plans—especially those presented to the electorate by political leaders. Thus, for example, I unhappily believe that it is probable that Japan will be compelled to make excessive efforts to sell its goods abroad because the successful candidate for re-election in 1963, Hayato Ikeda, pledged his administration to achieve an annual cumulative growth rate of seven per cent. To attain this Japan will have to increase its imports of raw materials, processed goods and specialized machinery substantially.

There is another wish—or preference—which the American government would like to express through its foreign aid program: that the people of recipient countries should observe democratic self-governing political methods.[8]

This preference rests on a belief in their superiority and a notion that the spread of democracy will benefit the United States. Most Americans hold the opinion that peoples can live in freedom and with personal dignity only when they are self-governing and equals under the law. They are inclined to respond more readily to requests for aid made by those governments which share these political ideas than those made by others. The shared conception of what are seemly political practices is a bond. Most Americans also believe that in the long run political democracies will be more progressive and creative, hence more likely to be able to master poverty and go forward. Moreover, in the American experience, self-governing countries have usually proved to be stauncher and more reliable friends and allies than others.

Some students of foreign policy and foreign aid believe there is another more trenchant reason for favoring countries where political democracy and popular control over foreign policy prevail. They believe such countries are more nearly immune from the frenzies that lead to war than others. But history leaves this opinion in doubt. It is denied not only by spokesmen for other types of political society but by some observant Western diplomats and historians. The dissenters lament the exercise of popular control

8. I have shirked the task of defining "political democracy" with precision. There are various types and degrees which shade into each other, and in some of which democratic ways and institutions are mingled with those of oligarchy or dictatorship. An attempt at classification of the type of political systems in the Afro-Asian countries can be found in the concluding essay in the collection entitled *The Politics of the Developing Areas*, edited by Gabriel A. Almond and James A. Coleman, pages 561–563. A classification of systems is suggested; political democracy (as in the Philippines); tutelary democracy (as in Indonesia); terminal colonial democracy (as in Nigeria); modernizing oligarchy (as in Pakistan), colonial or racial oligarchy (as in Southern Rhodesia) and traditional oligarchy (as in Ethiopia). But the authors recognize that the distinctions between these may be fine and the characteristics mingled.

over foreign policy and the call which it makes for "open diplomacy." They believe it a mistake to require the officials who conduct foreign affairs to consult and please the populace, contending that this compels diplomats to be either prudent panderers or clever deceivers of their own people. For if, with skilled and calm professional judgment, the directors of foreign policy seek to rise above national feeling in the quest for peace or justice, they will be badgered or discharged.

The task of sorting out the historical evidence on this subject would challenge the philosophical insight of a Plato. It might even humble a Toynbee with his vast memory, amassed files, and delight in bold generalizations. All dictators save a very few have paid more homage to power and less homage to ideals of peace and justice than have democratic leaders. But in times of intense crisis, they may exercise more effective check on popular passions and fears than can democratic leaders. Or they may make these feelings more explosive. Certainly governments run by rapacious and unbalanced corsairs like Napoleon, Hitler, Mussolini, and Mao Tse-tung will sooner or later bring about war. But sober and responsible monarchs or ruling groups—military or civilian—may be genuine peace-seekers and peace-makers.

Whatever the validity of this particular reason for regarding the observances of democracy as a preferred qualification for aid, other grounds are sufficient. However, they are not a conclusive indicator of the merits of a country or of its ability to progress, or of the trend of its future association with the United States. Hence, while being a pertinent affecting circumstance, our decisions to give or refuse aid should not be subjected to the limiting stipulation that only democracies need expect fair consideration.

It would be self-defeating to require any and all governments that seek American aid to adopt, at once and at our behest, the forms and methods of democracy. Some of the peoples most in need of help are so illiterate, dispersed and divided that their progress toward democracy must wait on other preliminary changes. Some nations by temperament and tradition seem able to manage their affairs better under some form of personal rule from above—monarchy, or a self-appointed head or council. This is more or less true of many countries in Latin America and the Middle and Far East. In these the interest in constitutional government as an ideal and as a practical form is weak; the willingness to observe the rules and limits of party politics is wavering; and the respect for law is less than for personal authority. As and when education spreads and industrial growth may bring into existence a larger and more secure middle class, this may change. But in the near future the aims of the American aid program may, in such countries, be better served by a firm but public-spirited government which can ably direct public affairs than by a wobbly and infirm party government.

Did not Turkey arise under Ataturk, and then move on toward a semi-republican form of government? Would Pakistan now be better off if Ayub Khan had not taken over from a broken-down party government? Would Iran progress more rapidly if the Shah were displaced by an Assembly dominated by large landowners or Communists? What will happen in Jordan if King Hussein is displaced by passionate Arab politicians or military men?

The American administrators of aid have accommodated themselves to such facts and uncertainties. Their course has been pragmatic. In some cases they have reconciled themselves to supporting a dictatorial government because the preceding democratic one had been so distracted by party rivalries that it could not carry out elementary duties or make essential reforms. In other instances they have come to the aid of a self-appointed military or political combination because there was a grave danger that Communists, or Communists and Fascists in combination, would gain control of the democratic machinery of government and degrade it. In yet others, aid has been extended because the American officials concluded that the governing group which had assumed power, though undemocratic, were honest, capable and concerned with public welfare. In still others, aid was forthcoming because the regime in power was willing to accord the United States military or strategic facilities. And lastly, there have been situations and occasions when an obvious attempt was made to use our power to grant or deny aid to compel the person or group who was in control of a foreign government—the sovereign, general, military ruler, tribal head, or civilian dictator—since popular rule would have only alienated them and failed.

For one or several of these reasons the American government has given and is giving aid and support to many countries that are governed autocratically—among them Spain, Portugal, Yugoslavia, Pakistan, the United Arab Republic, Jordan, Morocco, Algeria, Iran, Iraq, Ethiopia, Ghana, Thailand, Taiwan and South Korea.

However, toward countries it thinks it can effectively influence, and in accord with the desires of their people, the American government has been using its control over the provision of aid actively to support the call for democratic civilian rule against autocracy—especially military autocracy. It did so, for example, in South Korea in April 1963. President Kennedy, taking the risk of being blamed by Koreans for dictating to them and of alienating the military, let it be known that the American government was about to reduce economic aid to that country. The action was timed to influence the course and outcome of discussions between the military group which had taken control of the government and civilian politicians—to give point to the hope, in the phrase used by President Kennedy that ". . . a situation will develop which will permit the blossoming of democratic rule—responsible and stable government in South Korea." [9]

But it is in the American hemisphere, especially, that the government of the United States has been trying to make the political wind, not merely to tack into it. At the mast it has been flying a

9. A report from Seoul in *The New York Times* of April 4, 1963, by A. M. Rosenthal was a lucid account of the essential features of the situation in South Korea at that time, and the American relation to it. President Kennedy's comments were made at his press conference of April 3, 1963.

pennant bearing the pledge to which the American government subscribed along with those of the Latin American countries at Punta del Este—to improve and strengthen democratic institutions.

In this cause the American government in 1962 made known that it would end all help to the Dominican Republic if a group that had been associated with Trujillo's dictatorship took over the government of that country, at the same time deploying naval forces to deter them from trying. The direct action succeeded. Most of the Latin American countries applauded it. Not even those governed by military juntas complained of "Intervention" or "Imperialism."

But the next attempt to defend democracy by the exercise of our power to give or deny economic help was abortive. In Peru, in July-August 1962, popular elections, challenged as fraudulent, had opened the way to power for a combination of political parties in which the distinctly radical elements were dominant. A military junta ejected the President from office and called off the scheduled meeting of the Peruvian Congress which was to have elected his successor. The leaders were a few of the many Latin American officers who had been trained in American military academies in the expectation that they would come to like our ways and admire our standards, and so want their countries to steer a political course akin to ours.[10]

10. Our willingness to welcome Latin American soldiers, sailors and airmen in our schools and training centers was candidly explained by Secretary of Defense MacNamara in order to convince Congress that the expense was justified: "Probably the greatest return on our military assistance investment comes from the training of selected officers and key specialists at our military schools and training centers in the United States and overseas. These students are hand-picked by their countries to become instructors when they return home. They are the coming leaders, the men who will have the know-how and impart it to their own forces. I need not dwell upon the value of having in positions of leadership men who have first-hand knowledge of how Americans do things and how they think. It is beyond price to us to make friends of such men." Statement of Secretary of Defense MacNamara submitted to Subcommittee on Appropriations of House of Representatives, March 16, 1962; Hearings, vol. 1, page 359.

The Peruvian junta could honestly allege that their action was in accord with some American precepts. As citizens and as officers, was it not their duty to prevent disorder, avert what they alleged to be minority rule, and keep irresponsible elements out of places of influence until they, the real guardians of the people, could create conditions under which an honest popular choice could be made? These reasons they could and did give for disregarding the American tradition and rule that military men must not interfere in political affairs. The head of the junta, General Godoy, hastened to announce that he wished Peru to continue to be a participant in the Alliance for Progress; and he called upon Peruvians, "to make an unprecedented effort to solve our national problem and bring about the well-being of all . . . This effort, carried out with technique and spirit," he added, "should attract the promised aid of the Alliance for Progress which is the most positive measure of social and economic justice and, therefore, of effective combat against Communist infiltration." [11]

Despite these defenses and avowals, the American government thought it must prove to the people of Latin America that it was as opposed to the seizure of power by conservative military elements as by conspiratorial radical ones. Maybe it feared that if it did not take a definite stand at once toward Peru, military groups in Argentina and Brazil, even then interventors in the chaotic political struggles within their countries, might similarly elevate themselves, ending the prospect of democratic rule; and similar possibilities loomed elsewhere—in Ecuador, and perhaps even in Venezuela. Whatever his reasons, the President announced in haste that the American government was suspending all economic aid to Peru and ordered American technicians who were working with Peruvian authorities on projects under the sponsorship of the Alliance for Progress to stay away from their jobs. These admonitory measures were all the more impressive because the American government at the same time suspended diplomatic

11. *The New York Times,* July 20, 1962.

relations with Peru and halted military aid. In explanation, the White House stressed that in the Declaration adopted at Punta del Este the American nations had agreed in common, "to improve and strengthen democratic institutions through the application of the principle of self-determination by the people"; and that "in the case of Peru this great cause has suffered a serious setback." [12]

These abrupt and strong measures brought immediate and defensive responses. The junta deposed, and knowledgeable American observers thought with cause, that formerly much of American aid had not reached the people, having gone into the pockets of profiteers connected with the previous regime. It could give assurance that any future funds would reach those people in Peru who were "hungry and need aid." Soon after the junta began to allow the political parties to operate again. In rejoinder to President Kennedy's accusation, General Godoy declared: "We want to preserve democracy to have stability and tranquillity." To prove it sincerely the junta promised that within a few months another popular election would be held to choose the head of the government and that the military would then yield office to the people's choice.

In this interim signs appeared that although the other Latin American nations were pleased by this show of our resistance to military seizure of power, they disliked this open interference in the national affairs of one of their company. The ghost of American "intervention and imperialism" began to rise again. The echoes of old charges were heard once more. The American government concluded that since most of the Peruvian people seemed to have accepted the temporary rule of the junta, and in view of its promises to allow the return of constitutional government, it could with dignity rescind the measures taken. By promptly doing so it checked criticisms.

Still, in October 1963, in order to indicate its opposition to other

12. *Ibid.*

military coups that were occurring in Central America, and again to signal plainly its opposition to similar actions that might be in the offing elsewhere in Latin America, the American government peremptorily cancelled its aid programs for the Dominican Republic and Honduras and ordered all American economic and military advisers out of these countries. Secretary Rusk said it was doing so because, "under existing conditions . . . there is no opportunity for effective collaboration under the Alliance for Progress or for normalization of diplomatic relations."

Future historians will probably approve American action in these cases, and think it helped rather than hurt the American cause. However, experience continually shows how touch and go may be the results of attempts to require Latin American recipients of American aid to preserve the forms and procedures of democracy. The American government should pursue this purpose primarily by positive measures of assistance to constitutionally elected regimes which are genuinely striving to improve the condition of their people. These cannot be as easily distorted by internal Latin American politics.

It also (at a meeting in Panama with senior military officials of the countries joined in the Alliance for Progress) made an open effort to encourage military leaders to use their power to influence local political development toward the maintenance of constitutional government and social reform. The Americans stressed the desirability of combining vigilance against Communist subversion and oppressive dictatorship with vigorous efforts to lessen the causes of Latin American chronic political and social disorder: ignorance, poverty, injustice. In substance this means that the American government has accepted the probability that in many Latin American countries the local military forces will not infrequently play an active part in political events, and in crises a decisive one. The traditional American doctrine that military personnel and forces should be outside of politics is being supplemented by a conclusion that in Latin America and elsewhere, military leaders may have a responsibility to shape national life in a healthy and democratic way. I believe this to be a sensible adaptation. But the expectation that military leaders will be restrained in their ambitions and wise in judgment is likely to be disappointed as often as not.

Since the start of the century, the wheel of American policy has gone full circle and none of its quadrants has been free of trouble. Presidents Theodore Roosevelt, Taft, and Wilson all found themselves vilified as Yanqui imperialists because of their attempts to arrest political disorder and chaos in Latin-America and to install and uphold stable democratic regimes. Franklin D. Roosevelt concluded that no matter what financial or political plight a Latin-American country got into, our intervention was likely to turn out badly. During his terms of office the American government joined in a series of declarations and accords based on the principles of "equality of nations large and small" and "nonintervention." The cause of democracy in this hemisphere, he determined, should be upheld and advanced by cooperative efforts and by combined encouragement of a "good neighbor" rather than by castigation. But were he still alive, it is probable that he, too, would be disheartened by the present wave of political discord in so much of Latin America, and would feel compelled to stand ready to use our power to give or refuse aid whenever it might support or restore orderly democratic processes.

The task of discrimination and manipulation in behalf of democracy, as the American government pursues other purposes, would tax the wisdom of a Solomon and the shrewdness of Ben Franklin. But eager and bold younger men must substitute for them. They can only do their best, upheld by the knowledge that they are likely to be transferred or promoted, or to have resigned, before the consequences, good or bad, of their decisions become apparent.

Decisions about how to respond to requests for assistance from various kinds of political regimes are often made harder by incessant factionalism. Some of the poorest countries are more often than not in the throes of struggles for political power between groups not distinguishable by basic social aims or ideas.

When passing on otherwise meritorious requests for assistance from countries in which internal dissension is alive and constant, should the American government overlook that fact and respond favorably, or is it better advised to refuse or evade? If it gives the support asked, it risks the accusation by the opponents of the party and men in office that the United States is taking sides in their national affairs, and if and when the *out* group becomes the *in* group they may repudiate previous agreements and obligations. If on the other hand the American government, believing that the intense internal political battle will cause our efforts to aid to be futile, rejects otherwise sound requests, those in office will view the refusal as unfriendly or indicative of a wish to displace them. Such problems of decision are hard and are not easily reversible.

They are the more troublesome when the party in power is corrupt and incompetent; and/or treating its opponents harshly, cruelly. If the American government holds back until or unless the administration improves its ways—and accords a fair chance (in the American sense) to its critics and opponents, the foreign officials may take offense and raise the cry of "dictation." But if the American government decides that it is to mutual advantage to work with the group in office despite its faults, then, if the critics and opponents manage to overthrow the regime, they are likely to reprove us as having been indifferent to injustice and dishonesty. It may not be easy to calm them by explaining that if at the time of decision their country was to be helped at all, the United States had to deal with whatever regime was in power, and by doing so was not condoning its faults.

Up to now, almost all incoming administrations, after a while, have subordinated any ill-will they may have had because of our cooperation with their predecessors to the wish to secure a continuance of our help. But the United States cannot count on this propensity all the time everywhere. Thus caution and reserve are well advised toward regimes that do not have popular support or do not seem to be striving genuinely to serve the general good.

Regrettably strategic considerations will or must, in some situations, prevail over inclination. If any example is needed of the difficulty of decisions involved, that presented by the situation that developed in Vietnam in the summer of 1963 is a clear and important one. Having so deeply committed itself to the military and economic support of the regime of Ngo Dinh Diem to defeat Communist efforts to obtain control of the country, the American government was compelled to decide whether to suspend or continue it. Was it boldly to take the risks of suspending aid to the Diem regime until and unless it ejected its objectionable elements and arrived at a fair compromise with the Buddhist leaders and other opponents; the risks that the regime would be unable to continue to resist the Communists or be replaced by one which would not do so? Or was it to take the risks of continuing to support the regime despite its oppressive ways, its unpopularity, and its unsatisfactory conduct of the war against the Communists; the risks that despite our aid the regime would be repudiated by the people and lose the struggle against the Communists? Or was it to temporize, maintaining a critical aloofness but abstaining from a decisive and open break, as it continued to try to induce the Diem government to change its policies, or if it would not, wait for other groups—not unfriendly to the United States—to eject it from office?

Beset by contradictory reports and advice, President Kennedy during the summer vacillated. At one time he threatened to suspend aid unless American desires for change were satisfied. Then soon thereafter, yielding to the view that since the step might bring about a collapse in the regime, he announced, "it would not be helpful at this time" to reduce United States aid to South Vietnam.[13] And then finally in the autumn, as the reports of opposition and cruel oppression became more positive, he ordered the suspension of some kinds of support and aid for the regime—thereby

13. *The New York Times,* Sept. 9 and 10, 1963, and James Reston's column in the issue of Sept. 11 headed, "On Suppressing the News Instead of the Nhus."

signalling that it was probable that the American government would cooperate with rather than oppose any combination that ejected this regime from power, provided it would sustain the war against Communism.

By such quandaries is the American program of foreign aid harried because of global strategic concerns. They are putting to the test the question whether this country has not involved itself in too many remote situations which it cannot control.

12 | What Else to Ask of Recipients: Tolerable Posture in the Cold War

Some proponents of aid would have the American government unswervingly regulate its response to each petitioner by that nation's position in the struggle against international Communism—for us, or against us, or aloof. Congress, left to itself, might well have stipulated that the American government should require countries that want our aid to range themselves definitely on our side. Its inclination is indicated by the paragraph inserted in the Foreign Assistance Act of 1962:

> It is the sense of Congress that in the administration of these funds great attention and consideration should be given to those countries which share the view of the United States on the world crisis and which do not, as a result of the United States assistance, divert their own economic resources to military or propaganda efforts, supported by the Soviet Union or Communist China, and directed against the United States or against other countries receiving aid under this Act.

Sterner wishes gave way before the reasons why, for the very purpose in mind, the State Department had to have latitude. It has to interpret the outward mien and moves of each petitioner in the light of its internal situation and place in the congeries of nations. It ought to take into account all foreseeable reactions and consequences.

The political gyrations and gestures of some applicants for aid, especially the very poor and newly independent, may be neither consistent nor coherent. They may career back and forth, and crisscross, all within a few years. On some issues they may stand with the United States, on others be mute or elusive, on others oppose the United States.

Because of fear of endangering its existence in office, one government may evade all attempts to have it take sides openly. Another may think that by keeping the contestants guessing, it can levy on all. Another may really believe that people living in poverty cannot afford to choose between democratic capitalism and Communism and that it will make little difference to them under which system they live. Another may regard both systems as equally warlike, and so see no reason to attach itself to one rather than the other. These reasons, often intermingling, have affected the responses to our hints that if a needy country wants American help it had better tilt toward us.

The American government has sometimes been consistent, at other times inconsistent; firm in dealing with some countries, pliable in dealing with others.

Its announced general policy has undergone at least one major change. Early in his term as Secretary of State, John Foster Dulles publicly reproved all countries that professed to be neutral in the struggle between the West and the Communist bloc. Only those, he averred, which stood up to be counted on our side deserved our help. Others were to be left to make the best bargain they could for what they needed, or do without. For a while this line, coupled to American political alliances and strategic arrangements, was followed. But as time went on, exceptions and partial exceptions were made. Some were due to fear that countries who were turned down might draw closer to the Communist bloc. Thus, for example, the American government concluded that it would be self-defeating to stint India although it refused to align itself definitely with the United States. Other exceptions were due to the hope that countries helped by us despite their professions of neutrality, would be convinced that the United States respected their independence and that they would reciprocate American good-will. Then there were some governments whose real allegiance was hard to decipher those—for example, Egypt and Syria and Algeria—which, while insisting that they were not going to take sides in the cold war and while criticizing us and deferring to the Soviet Union, were stamping out Communist influence within their own borders; it was inferable that they felt safer to pose as critics rather than as friends of the West. Still other exceptions were prompted by the thought that habitual reliance on American aid might cause a beneficiary to become more respectful of our wishes in order to remain on the list.

It is hard to know when a country rejects our bid for thick-and-thin association whether, despite avowals that the United States will help reliable friends more than others, it believes that it is more likely to "come across" if it has to continue to woo them. Some countries have been swayed by the thought that the neutrality (or non-alignment) which kept open the door to Moscow would pay better than taken-for-granted support. This notion was entertained by some Latin American political leaders during the decade of the fifties, as they observed how much the United States was giving to India, the Middle East and Southeast Asia, and how comparatively little their own countries were receiving.

Governments may be adept at playing upon American anxieties. Their technique was once explained to me by a Latin American diplomat, as similar to that which he had perfected as a youth, when earning his school tuition as accompanist on the piano to a renowned but aging tenor. That singer was becoming unsure whether he could reach the high notes. One night, discerning that the tenor was trying but failing, the future diplomat dropped down a note or two in the scale as he was playing. The singer was grateful. The accompanist helped out again. The singer was grateful again. That rapport having been established, whenever the young man was in need of spending money, at the beginning of a concert he started on a higher note than the one marked on the score, then, after a meaningful glance, earned a reward by lowering the pitch.

To those African and Southeast Asian countries which have recently emerged from under the tutelage or control of one of the imperialisms of the West, free will, self-rule are hard won and exciting attainments. Some are apt to regard implied political conditions for aid as a renewal of bondage even though they might merely be expressive of equal association in and for a common cause. Most have been averse to entering into any firm political commitments with the West. They have professed that rather than do so they would get along as best they could without American aid, and a few hinted that they would respond to Moscow's offers to give help without strings.

The political leaders of some petitioners for aid have condoned their coldness by their state of extreme need as, for example, did Sylvanus Olympio, the late and to-be-lamented President of Togo: "We cannot afford to be involved in the cold war with all its consequences. The African peoples are at the lowest stage of economic growth and should wisely devote all their energies and resources to the development of their peoples." [1]

A curious extension of the idea that poverty, in itself, is a reason for not taking sides in the cold war, was propounded by ex-President Janio Quadros of Brazil, as a defense against American criti-

1. Article, "African Problems in the Cold War," in *Foreign Affairs*, Oct., 1961.

cism of his declared intention to improve Brazil's relations with the Soviet Union and enlarge Brazil's trade with the Communist bloc:

> We cannot too often stress the extent to which poverty separates us from North America and the leading European countries of the Western World. If by their success these represent, in the eyes of undeveloped peoples, the ideal of achievement of the elite of European cultural origin, there is none the less taking root in the mind of the masses the conviction that this ideal, for a country without resources and hamstrung in its aspirations for progress is a mockery. What solidarity can there be between a prosperous nation and a wretched people? . . . Thinking of this sort irrevocably creates in us a sense of solidarity with those poverty-stricken peoples who, on three continents, are struggling against imperialist interests, which under the umbrella of democratic institutions—mislead—if not destroy—attempts to organize popular economics." [2]

Such avowals as this and that of his successor, Goulart, who was not as explicit, are in effect claims that the American government should continue to assist any country that is poor just because it is poor, even though it deprecates the issues between democracy and despotism, and cultivates relations with our adversaries. [3]

Enunciations of attitude toward attempts to connect foreign aid with natural posture in the cold war can be confusing and contradictory. Examples of how they may be abound.

To recall one, at the very time President Kwame Nkrumah of Ghana in Washington in late September, 1961 was asking help

2. "Brazil's New Foreign Policy," in *Foreign Affairs*, Oct., 1961.
3. Report of President Goulart's televised news conference in Santiago, Chile, April 24, 1963, in *The New York Times*, April 25, 1963. An excerpt read: "Asked about Brazil's so-called neutral foreign policy, Mr. Goulart said neutralism gives the impression of a static attitude whereas Brazil's policy is dynamic. Brazilian policy is geared to the idea of freedom and self-determination of people and is absolutely independent of the big military blocs." Is he confused, or merely confusing?

to construct a great dam and power plant on the Volta River, his Foreign Minister, Ako Adjer, was declaiming in the General Assembly of the United Nations:

> The colonial powers realize that the time has come for them to concede independence to the African people. However, they try every device to deprive the African states of the real substance and meaning of their economic and cultural agreements and the granting of scientific and technical advice.[4]

To recall another, when past and continuing American contributions to the military strength and economic life of a recipient were dismissed as a reason for leaning toward the West, as it was by Foreign Minister Mohammad Ali of Pakistan, after the Chinese-Indian clash. Be assured, he told the members of the National Assembly that:

> The government is fully prepared to tap all resources irrespective of which country it may be, to improve our position. . . . That should give a clear indication of the positive independent line we are adopting—the criterion being what is in the best interests of Pakistan, not what suits others. . . . There is no eternal friendship in international relations and there is no eternal enmity. . . . In the national interest we shall make friends—whoever is interested to accept our hand. If friends let us down, we shall no longer consider them as friends. Friends that stand by us we will stand by.[5]

Even more examples of apparent perversity are in the record. As when, just after asking President Kennedy for aid in dealing with the profound economic problems of his country, and while discussions of an aid program were in prospect, Premier Ben Bella of Algeria signed a joint communiqué with Castro in which the two expressed an identity of views, and supported Castro's demand that the United States give up its naval base on Guantanamo Bay. Presumably Ben Bella took pleasure in thus thumbing

4. *The New York Sunday Times Magazine*, Oct. 6, 1961.
5. *The New York Times*, Nov. 23, 1962.

his nose at the affluent patron. Probably his real reason for doing so was to keep Communist-inclined elements in his country from forsaking his leadership for that of more extreme and avid political rivals. His action may have been so construed in Washington. For while the State Department was irked, it went out of its way to explain that formal economic discussions had not begun and that the American government would continue to supply emergency food and medical relief to [Algerian] refugees and the homeless.

These instances suffice to suggest how restrained the American government has been in its rebuttals of offensive generalities about American purposes and policies, hoping that soft answers would turn away wrath. Successive administrations have judged it to be more advantageous as well as more humane to include even outspokenly critical countries in the American foreign aid programs rather than leave them in extreme need. They have ceased to condemn and have been lenient toward countries whose attitude in and toward the cold war has been vacillating or inclined away from us. Thus the American government has continued to make large grants and loans to India, the United Arab Republic, Iraq, Morocco, Algeria, and even to Ghana and Indonesia.

The working premises on which the American government has been acting were candidly and lucidly stated by Secretary of State Rusk:

> Insofar as our attitude toward neutrals are concerned [*sic*] this is getting into something of a quagmire because there are many neutrals, and there is nothing very solid about the only thing they seem to have in common, and that is that they do not happen to be aligned either to the Sino-Soviet bloc nor to the so-called Western bloc. So there are many shades of opinion and attitude among the so-called neutrals.
>
> They will say things from time to time which will annoy us. They will take points of view on particular questions which differ from ours. They will criticize us specifically on certain points, sometimes in the most vigorous terms. But the test is whether they are determined to be independent, whether they are trying

to live out their own lives in the way in which their own people would like to have them to shape it.

To the extent that this is so, then I think we can afford to have the patience of a great power, to have the persistence of a country that is thinking about the shape of the world twenty-five years from now, and not allow ourselves to be upset on a day-to-day or week-to-week basis by a particular point of view on a particular question. The stakes are too high for that.[6]

This way of treating stand-offish recipients recently won the conditional assent of the Clay Committee, which observed:

> . . . aid to countries which are avowedly neutral and sometimes critical of us may be in order, as long as their independence is genuine, their over-all behavior responsible, and the use of their own resources prudent and purposeful.

This course and the reasons for maintaining it were reaffirmed by President Kennedy in response to suggestions made prior to the Chinese advances into northern India that the aid to that country be suspended if it went on with negotiations with the Soviet Union for the establishment of a factory to make combat airplanes.

> I think we have to make a judgment as to what serves our interest, whether the country is attempting to maintain its freedom; whether the country is pursuing policies which are not inimical to the long-range interests of the United States. We make that independent judgment on each occasion.[7]

This policy is, of course, a gamble on our powers to please and impress. One or more of these professedly unaligned countries may later turn against the United States on some crucial issue. Or even sign up with its enemies because it came to dislike us more, or as part of an economic bargain, or because it concluded that the Communists were going to be the winners. Against such

6. Press Conference, Nov. 17, 1961.
7. Press Conference, Aug. 23, 1962.

contingencies our buffers are our own strength and shock-resistant capabilities. The United States seeks companions; but it is not to be a courtier.

To intrude my own comment, I think the American government would be justified in insisting when the question at issue is really important, that countries that want substantial American assistance should not oppose the American position. They can hardly expect us to help them make their own future brighter while they darken ours. Whether or not acknowledged, American protection is enabling them to be independent and aloof. The strength of the West is their shield against coercive Communist demands and unwanted intrusion.

This point was sharply outlined at the Punta del Este Conference in 1961. The American delegation sought to have Cuba excluded from the Organization of American States and to persuade all the other members to impose an embargo on trade with Cuba similar to the one maintained by the United States. These proposals were opposed by some of the other members on two scores; that they would punish Cuba for being independent; that they would be a form of intervention to compel Cuba to conform to the ideas of the United States and benefit private American interests.

Secretary of State Rusk strove to offset these distortions of our reasons for seeking to isolate Cuba by stressing that the Castro government was being imposed on the Cuban people and being kept in power only by external Communist support. He stressed that "Security from extra-continental intervention is essential to the success of our cooperative efforts to achieve social and economic advancement under the Alliance for Progress." This observation was well taken. The Communists and their sympathizers in all Latin American countries were doing their utmost to prevent the joint program for economic progress from getting well under way, and was combining with any other elements—reactionary or despotic, who wanted it to fail.

Cuba was at this meeting voted out of the OAS. But many of the Latin American countries continued to trade with Cuba. The American government did not suspend aid to any of them. But Congress was exasperated and showed it in its treatment of the next appropriations for the Alliance for Progress.

That the President had been well advised not to have tried to compel the other members of the OAS against their will to cut off trade with Cuba became clear in the critical autumn of 1962. *All* the Latin American governments then stood with the United States in its demand that the Soviet government take its long-range missiles and bombing planes out of Cuba. Evidently all had come to perceive that the real issue was not Cuban independence and immunity from American dictation but their own protection against the Communist conspiracy and the need for joint resistance.

Even more of a deviation from the straight line of political preference have been the substantial loans and sales for local currencies to two members of the Communist bloc—Yugoslavia and Poland.

American aid to Tito started in 1950 after the Central Committee of the Communist Party of the Soviet Union reprimanded him for insubordination and ordered all members of the Communist bloc to reduce trade with Yugoslavia. Tito stopped conniving with the Communist guerillas in Greece, making it possible to end the civil war in that country. Soon thereafter drought in Yugoslavia made famine imminent. President Truman recommended and Congress approved large consignments of surplus food to be paid for in Yugoslav currency "to prevent the weakening of the defenses of the Federal Peoples' Republic of Yugoslavia."

What was then begun as emergency relief burgeoned during the next decade as regular support for Tito's effort to maintain in Yugoslavia a state-directed economy less intolerant than the Russian model, and not subservient to Russian orders. If he were allowed to fail for lack of means to pay for imported essentials, he would be compelled to come to heel. If that happened, no other member of the Communist group in Europe, it was thought, would ever again dare display a will of its own. Conversely, if American aid enabled the Yugoslav people to progress as fast or faster than Soviet subjects, they would support Tito and he would be able to act independently.

The more optimistic even conceived that the liaisons formed might alter the image that the Yugoslav ruler had of capitalist personalities and purposes; and that this, along with American demonstrated good will, might lead Tito to moderate the international Communist assault on the West, or even to side with the West when Moscow pushed too hard. For the United States would be showing that its diplomacy was defensive, that it was not ruled by fixed hatred of any and all social systems based on state control of economic life.

But so far American aid has not had these salutary results. Tito has shown himself adept at procuring aid from both the United States and the Soviet Union without causing either to conclude that it was wasting their money. He has been reported to have acted as tutor to other scheming heads of states, particularly Nasser, in the arts of extraction.[8] He has turned up on the Communist side at the telling hour of every tense controversy with the West. Particularly in September 1961, at the meeting of the heads of "neutral" or "unaligned" countries, he roughly shocked American opinion. Taking offense at what he construed as an American attempt to test his attachments and intentions, and provoked by a pause in American sales of surplus foodstuffs to Yugoslavia for local currencies, he accused the American government of using economic pressure in an effort to force Yugoslavia to change its foreign policy. In words warmed by wrath he praised the policies and views which the Soviet government had recently stated in the Twenty-second Congress of Communist Parties, declaring

8. Article by Cyrus L. Sulzberger in *The New York Times*, June 19, 1962.

bluntly: "But we will not yield whether the United States give us aid or not."

The State Department did not take open affront at Tito's expressions of approval of Soviet policies and his belittling of what the United States had done for his people. It made known that it was ready to discuss the resumption of food sales. However, Congress concluded that our course had been based on false premises and unwarranted expectations. To cut off the flow of aid to Yugoslavia and Poland, it stipulated in the Foreign Assistance Act of 1962 that no assistance should be given any Communist country; and the President was forbidden to waive this restriction unless he ". . . finds and promptly reports to Congress that (1) such assistance is vital to the security of the United States; (2) the recipient country is not controlled by the international Communist conspiracy; and (3) such assistance will further promote the independence of the recipient country from international Communism."

Were Cagliostro in the White House, he would not be able to demonstrate these three points convincingly to skeptics. However, the President and the State Department took the responsibility of finding that the conditions laid down by Congress were met. Sales of foodstuffs to Yugoslavia for local currencies were resumed though on different terms than before. Whether or not because of the wish not to lose our aid and trade, Tito subsequently seemed to profess again a genuine wish for friendly association with us. Suppositions, already described, are once again propping up the opinion that the United States would be well advised to continue to aid the Yugoslav people. Because of the less openly hostile phase of the cold war that followed the American-Soviet-British accord upon banning tests of atomic weapons, Tito's subsequent reconciliation with Khrushchev, transient or lasting, has not refreshed American opposition to a continuation of assisting activities.

The train of thought and purpose which led the American government to give substantial economic aid to the Polish Communist government is similar to that which influenced our treatment of Yugoslavia. But other considerations have also influenced the decision. Numerous family connections still exist between Poles in Poland and their relatives in the United States. Most Poles are devout Catholics. The belief or faith lingers that they as a people and a nation are irrepressibly independent and feel basically that they belong with the West, not to the Soviet realm. Moreover, the sense prevails that the Polish authorities, when and if the question of a thermonuclear war should become immediate, would urge compromise.

American aid to Poland has been the token of confidence in these conjectures. But the United States should not be taken wholly aback if its aid is acknowledged, at some time or other, as were the gifts sent by the British government, seeking to curry favor, to the King of Ashanti—a gilt chair, a velvet robe, a candelabrum, a box of wax candles, two cases of brandy.

The King, not to be outdone, informed the representative of His Majesty's Government: "I send you one small tiger by my messenger."

The American people invest in, give to, instruct, and prod needy foreign countries because they believe it will advantage our national security and reputation as well as satisfy our sense of decency. Even though the United States may sometimes be meanly repaid, it should continue to be open-handed rather than tight-fisted. It must not allow its activities in aid to be either deformed or rotted by fright. It must not again act and speak as though it visualized its position to be that of the supporting member of an acrobatic team in a circus; standing on the extended arms of a massively muscled man, a pyramid of other men are tremulously poised; if any one of those aloft wavers, all come tumbling down on top of the strong man. In such a structure the safety of all members of the troupe can be vitally hurt by the faltering of any one member. The United States is not crucially dependent in that way, and must not give the impression of believing that it is.

But the United States wants associates in order to end the abominable contest that is now dividing the world by mutual tolerance —time-tempering tolerance—rather than by trial in battle. It would like all nations to have a fair chance to improve their conditions of life and work, in orderly freedom, without compulsion from outside or social strife within. These should be, if they are not, the messages conveyed by the clangor of foreign aid.

We must not ever assume that our economic aid in and of itself can assure friendship or even reliable impartiality. It will not do so if our character deteriorates, if our life is riven by divisions between blacks and whites, workers and employers, city and country; if we do not maintain armed forces strong enough to cause enemies to pause; if our diplomacy is not adroit, reasonable and appealing. Dollars must be a symbol of American vigor and magnanimity, and not a signal of military or diplomatic dependence. By appearance and act the United States must keep or win the respect of the mature and excite the imagination of the young in other nations.

Thus, mindful of Machiavelli's admonition in *The Prince* that "The friendship which is gained by purchase and not through grandeur and nobility of spirit is bought but not secured," our ability to aid others will signify our decent greatness and make them be proud of our company.

But as in the past, exceptions to these lofty attitudes will have to be made when dealing with countries from which the United States wants to get rights or opportunities of military value to itself or its allies. For these it may be sensible to pay in one way or another. Military pacts are seldom, if ever, practical arrangements of limited significance. Those who accord rights to us may expose themselves to greater risk of engagement in war, suffering, destruction. Associates in military arrangements, especially in those which provide for the use of bases or ports or the stationing of American forces within their territories, or for contingent joint or combined strategies or commands, merge their national destinies with ours to an unpredictable extent.

This creates an obligation beyond military aid or cooperation. Like the wish that led to the accord, the obligation is mutual, and contains implicitly an expectation of reciprocal economic aid and political support. Gratifyingly, it may be noted that aid given for military reasons has contributed to the economic improvement and social welfare of some main allies.

The aid that the United States gives in connection with agreements for military cooperation must reflect the vagaries of circumstances in a world divided as it is at present. Tied to it is, or should be, the requirement that the United States gets what it bargains for—cooperation in the struggle for power and military superiority in the strife against Communism.

Part four |

DILEMMAS AND
DECISIONS

13 | Dilemmas Due to the Quirks of International Politics

If universities bestowed honorary degrees of "Doctor of Dilemmas" those engaged in directing American foreign aid should have them.

Of all those dilemmas encountered, the most pervasive and recurrent are those that arise in the determination of *who* is to get *what* and *how much*. The total requests of foreign governments are always much more than the sum that Americans are disposed to provide and Congress to appropriate.

The relative allocations cannot be settled by inflexible standards or solely by scrupulous moral principles. The facts and national purposes which must be considered apropos of each request are different in kind and variable. Impartial rules of equality, the dues of friendship, the desire to reward character and capacity— all are subject to the changes in American national necessities, real or fancied.

All allotments must be fitted into the total sum made available for distribution among the many applicants. What is accorded to each may be scaled up or down according to its attendant relations with the United States and its readiness to conform to the stipulations which the American government may attach to its aid—such as "self-help."

When the program for a country is propelled by the wish to assuage social discontent and thereby forestall internal Communist subversion, its dimensions are determined by the anticipated cost of stimulating a substantial and sustained improvement —as it was under the Marshall Plan and as under the Alliance for Progress.

When deemed vital to increase a country's income rapidly to enable it to carry the burden of maintaining large military forces, the amounts (formerly called "supporting assistance") allowed are measured on the scale of urgency rather than on the scale of economic reason.

When the aid is in reality a payment for specific military facilities as, for example, in the case of Morocco, Spain, Portugal and Ethiopia, the amounts allowed are measured on the scale of bargaining.

When the sums are awards to encourage and enable a country to manage without obligating itself to the Communist bloc, the amounts provided are adjusted to the depths of need, and the degree of probability that either the government in power or those who seek to eject it from office would sell national independence to the Communists for economic aid.

At the end of each annual affray with Congress over appropriations for foreign aid the Executive has viewed the outcome with anguish. For no matter how solid and well evidenced the reasons for our offers of aid may be, how genuine our avowals of goodwill, it is impossible for American officials to convince all foreign petitioners that they have been treated as fairly and generously as American national circumstances justify. Laments, often loud and lively, are strewn in the records.

During the years when by far the largest sums were being allocated to countries which were members of the Marshall Plan, the Latin American countries thought that they were being neglected. Now that much more is being set aside for them, some African and Middle Eastern countries are carping at the refusal of the American government to give them more, and insinuating that it was because they will not take orders from the United States.

Noting what was being done for Turkey, India and Pakistan, the Shah of Iran complained in 1962 that his country, in comparison, was being meanly treated. Was it not standing up against the Communist menace at greater risk than they, he asked? Were not he and his government, then headed by Ali Amini, trying hard to reduce the budget deficit, shrink the bureaucracy, and partition land ownership? When, in the face of those claims to consideration, our government refused to give Iran enough to maintain too large an army, the Prime Minister resigned, averring in his farewell statement that our treatment of his country was all the more unfair because "Iran is America's only sincere friend in this part of the world." [1] The Shah and the new Prime Minister decided to content themselves with less—when reminded that the Iranian Treasury was receiving about three hundred million dollars a year out of the earnings of the oil companies in which American interests were dominant, and was being enabled thereby to finance one of the greatest hydro-electric and irrigation power schemes in the world. The Shah may or may not have noted that during this same time of complaint, the President of Pakistan was disparaging what was being done for his country as compared with India and Iran.

One more example of the troubles of apportionment: The Israeli authorities have let it be known, now and then, that they thought the aid given their country by the American government was less than its due when its needs, capabilities, exposed position, and fidelity to Western ideals were taken into account. Concurrently, the Arab countries, except a few oil-rich ones, were deploring what they thought to be the favor shown to Israel.

1. *The New York Herald Tribune,* July 19, 1962.

The American government has made a patient and considerate effort to correct disproportions not dictated by the exigencies of American diplomacy and strategy. It has usually had enough resources and ingenuity to enable it to ward off lastingly adverse effects on its relations with any aggrieved recipient. But not always; the sluggish response to the needs of Latin American countries lost the United States influential friends in some of these countries and caused some other friends to lose influence with their people.

There is no way in which this kind of dilemma, or rather this portfolio of dilemmas, can be disposed of once and for all. There never will be an accepted code of aid set by tradition or convention to which all the needy or discontented will defer. There is no impartial arbiter in this area of operation. There is no monitor who can reprimand complainants who are trying to test the truth of the proverb that "the axle that squeaks the loudest gets the most grease."

Those who have the task of allocation must convince, reconcile and appease any worthy claimants who believe themselves neglected. They must mollify such others as may try to pry out of the United States more than is justified, even while deferring or denying American requests. Figuratively, the American government must manage like the old lady who lived in a shoe and had so many children she did not (at times) know what to do.

The greatest disparities in the distribution of American aid among the many countries which need or want it have been caused by the exigencies of the cold war. Thus, to support its military accords and plans, the American government has given some poor countries far more aid than they would have earned by their economic or social needs, or merits, or the size of population as compared with others. In the past, countries which for this reason have been given far more aid than was otherwise their due include Greece, Turkey and the Philippines. Recently they included South Korea, Taiwan, Vietnam, Laos, Cambodia, and Thailand. In these our economic aid is complementary to active military protection and support. On or near the defended borders of all six of the small Asian countries named stand large Communist armies. Native elements have been indoctrinated, trained, organized and equipped by the Russian or Chinese or Vietminh Communist governments. All would have fallen before the Communist assaults and appeals had not the United States upheld them, equipping their military forces, providing their people with food, teaching them better ways of farming, and providing the means for building roads and airfields, as well as transport and industrial equipment. The American government has tried to compensate not only for their deficiencies but their failings.

The United States is gambling in each case that sooner or later the Communists will be compelled to recognize that they cannot win and then some settlement will be made that assures these protected beneficiaries the chance to live in safety and freedom. Should any or all of them succumb to the Communist assault or allure, the economic growth nurtured by us would redound to the benefit of the Communists. This risk of such an occurrence is at the present time still substantial for South Korea and Taiwan and menacing in Vietnam. For despite the hundreds of millions of dollars the United States has expended to support them, none has yet developed an economy that is viable or a government that can count on lasting and firm popular support and resistance to Communism.

By pointing out these disproportions and risks, I do not mean to insinuate that they should not be borne. But they are reasons why the American government must continuously make clear that American support is contingent on vigorous and courageous devotion of the recipients to avowed mutual causes and responsive to its advice. It should not wait, as it did in the case of Cambodia, until its aid is rejected and ejected.

Another disproportion in our allocations of aid is due to the wish to avert conflicts such as those which have recurred in the Congo; conflicts between local tribes and/or leaders which might turn into greater wars.

The numerous separate tribal groups who live within the boundaries of what was formerly the Belgian Congo do not have and do not feel any strong unifying connections with one another. The Belgian colonial administration held them together under its rule but did not bring them into close daily association in commerce, or in social organization or education or government or by building roads. Left alone, the Congo would probably split into two, three or four separate states. That would bring tumult, suffering and internal disorder, rivalries, and perhaps war which might spread over adjoining areas. Foreign intervention would be invited, and would probably ensue. For one or other of its fragments, poor and weak, might, if its leaders were inclined that way or had no other resource, beseech the Communist bloc for support while others would look to the West for support. Then the United States might find itself compelled to expend more in funds and in men than it is now doing.

Hence the resolve of the American government and its associates in the United Nations to maintain the authority of the Central Congo government and to assist it to extend its authority over all the provinces. Hence the admitted, reluctantly admitted, necessity of supporting its army, relieving distress in the towns and countryside, assisting it to create the elements of tenable administrative and economic systems. But grave doubts remain whether the federal government can survive and unify the country. Ironically in 1964 as revolts again spread through the provinces, the American government asked the Belgian government to persuade Belgian industrialists, technicians and advisers to use their former connections to stimulate the economy and end the civil war.

I turn from the dilemma of disproportion to that of diversion. Ordinarily, the American government can see to it that the aid it provides for a specified economic or social project is used in the designated way. But it is often hard, and sometimes impossible, to guard against unforeseen and undesirable "side effects"—to borrow an expression used about the new drugs. The American government often tries to obtain assurances from governments of impoverished recipients of aid given to improve economic conditions that they will not defeat this purpose by maintaining military forces greater than are needed either for national defense or policing. But it is not easy to persuade those who have different ideas and wishes to defer to the judgment of the United States. For there is no precise and generally recognized line marking the size of the military force which a country is justified in maintaining. In this stormy field, each flag waves alone.

The American government has seldom tried direct economic coercion to compel a poor country to desist from needless enlargement of its military forces. It has been afraid that if it tried, willful political or military heads might, as happened, turn to the Communist bloc for the economic aid it was refused by the United States, and for weapons as well. It has stood by, albeit watchfully, for example, while India and Pakistan and most of the Arab states of the Middle East and North Africa, all deeply in need of American aid to progress materially, use up much of their meager resources in a competitive construction of their military power.

But in one flagrant situation the patience of Congress grew exhausted, and the opinion that the results of its aid had been perverted, prevailed. A provision was inserted in the current Foreign Assistance Act which required the termination of aid to any country that the President determines ". . . is engaging in or preparing for aggressive military efforts against the United States or any country receiving American aid . . ." This will disqualify the United Arab Republic. For it has been squandering the proceeds of its exports to the Soviet Union and American aid to pay for weapons bought from the Communist bloc, to employ German scientists to help create new war industries, to conduct military operations in Yemen, and to sustain a costly campaign of propaganda and conspiracy against Israel and Arab governments—those in Syria and Iraq—that have resisted Nasser's appeals.[2]

This provision will also disqualify Indonesia unless the government desists in its threats against Malaysia and curbs its ill-afforded military outlay.

By and large the American government has managed to minimize, though not entirely avert, this particular side effect of the assistance given to most Latin American countries. But it is getting harder to do so as Communist agents operating out of Cuba resort to every kind of agitation, conspiracy, sabotage. The efforts to check and frustrate these activities usually require an expansion of the local police forces. As the danger of Communist disturbances and assaults has become more serious even civilian governments have found it advisable to expand protective military organizations. And in several of the larger Latin American countries military leaders, declaring that the civilian governments were too weak, too hindered by party politics, or too leniently inclined toward Communism, have taken control of the government. When that happens, expenditure for military forces is likely to be incurred, and with it a diversion of domestic resources and foreign aid. Communist activity, in other words, forces the conversion of some of the means originally intended for economic growth into defense outlay. This is sometimes unavoidable but is always a regrettable setback.

In Saharan and sub-Saharan Africa similar diversions of assistance given for economic purposes are occurring. For in that region

2. The action of Congress was quickened by the informations and recommendation contained in the *Report of a Study of the United States Foreign Aid in Ten Middle Eastern and African Countries*, previously cited. After observing that "the United States is pouring its dollars into Egypt to help its economy while Egypt is pouring it out in foreign war" it was recommended that the continuation of the American financial aid program to Egypt be conditioned upon:

"(1) Egypt's prompt compliance with the terms of the United Nations settlement of the Yemen dispute;

(2) Egypt's reversal of her present armament policy so as to cease production of missiles, warplanes, submarines, and other implements of war clearly designed for aggressive purposes."

many boundaries, alliances, and tribal relations are not yet firmly settled. As ruefully remarked by one of the State Department representatives in the course of the hearings on the Military Aid Program in Africa, ". . . one of the things that happens when these countries become independent is that they do want to have some armed forces of their own." [3]

In existing circumstances, the American government should not and cannot follow too stiff a rule. But whenever it sensibly can be stubborn, it should be, especially when the foreign governments indulging in excessive military expenditure are aggressive or despotic in bent. It should make clear that by using up too much of their own resources this way they impair American inclination to help them in their struggle against poverty.

But it is easier to enunciate such advisory generalizations than to put them into practice. There have been and are situations where the expansion of a national military force serves the United States well in the cold war even though it increases the load on a poor nation.

No counsel in this matter can be wholly untinged by irony. For is not the United States spending more and more for its own military establishment? Is it now not urging many other members of NATO to increase their military contribution to that alliance against the Soviet Union? The extenuating reasons for this seeming inconsistency are well known and authentic. The military expenditures of the United States and its main allies are not voluntary and do not exceed what is needed to cause the Communists—who respect power alone—to be careful. They are a tremendous burden, borne for the protection of others as well as themselves. Moreover, the United States has the means of maintaining the required armed forces without itself suffering; it sacrifices no essentials of life and few comforts. Thus far this economically wasteful expenditure of its productive energies and resources has not

3. Henry J. Tasca, Deputy Assistant Secretary of State for African Affairs, Hearings, Subcommittee on Appropriations, House of Representatives, March 28, 1962.

caused any failure in the efforts to improve the American standard of living and social conditions. But poorer countries that need help can spare nothing for unproductive activities, and can contribute little to common defense.

The best evidence of our basic purpose is the sincerity of our efforts to bring to an end the competition in death-dealing power between the West and the Communist countries.

Most vexing of all dilemmas that originate and slither about in the meshes of American foreign policy are those that arise in the pursuit of several aims which rub against each other. This might be called the dilemma of "conflicting associations."

For example, as has been related, in 1962 the Kennedy Administration pleaded with Congress to be allowed to use its discretion in determining whether or not to continue aid to two members of the Communist bloc, Yugoslavia and Poland.

Yet—and this is the crux of the dilemma I am exposing—is there any real chance that either the Yugoslav or Polish Communist government—no matter how each evolves—will stand with the United States against Moscow in any crucial issue while the quarrel over the future of Berlin and Germany looms? For the way in which this dispute may be settled is more vital to their people than any change in material conditions. As long as they fear—as they do now—that American policy toward a restored Germany endangers their national territory or existence, the economic aid given them may be appreciated but it will not detach them from their powerful Soviet defender. Conceivably, however, association with them in their effort to better the condition of their people may cause them to take conciliatory actions that might lead to a settlement of the quarrel on terms which safeguard their security and lift the pall of thermonuclear war from Central Europe. And it may dispose them to stand the more steadfastly with the Soviet Union against the reckless fanaticism of Communist China.

Another type of criss-cross arises from friction between America's ideal of national independence and self-government and its obligations to some of its main allies in NATO. The American government has wanted to evince its sympathy for colonial peoples struggling for independence while retaining the amity of the mother countries. But, although its diplomacy has been nimble and its explanations soothing, it has not always managed to avoid giving offense to one or the other.

American relations with France were ruffled for years by such vexatious situations as French resentment at our provision of aid for Morocco and Tunis, who in turn were giving vital support to the Algerian rebels. This was one of the reasons why de Gaulle, aggrieved, refused to allow American ground, air and supply forces to remain on the bases in France. President Kennedy's expressed sympathy with the Algerian fight for independence is probably one of the unforgotten grudges which animates de Gaulle's present effort to lessen American influence in European affairs—which has upset soaring hopes of bringing all Western European countries into military and economic harmony with each other and with the United States.

Similarly, Holland was displeased by the continuation of aid to the Indonesian government when that clamorous regime was using force to compel the Dutch to turn over control of New Guinea. The Dutch government had to be convinced that if the United States showed a blank face and closed fist, the Indonesian rulers might enter into closer association with the Soviet Union. That particular dilemma was eased by the settlement that was finally mediated; but the memory of the fact that the United States had made it harder for Holland to regain and retain control of its former colonial empire in the Southwest Pacific is still alive.

A few harassing situations of the same sort remain. One may impair American relations with Portugal. Our air and naval bases in the Azores are of prime importance; therefore, the American government wishes to prolong the agreement with the Portuguese government which grants it the right to use them. Yet, in view of its professed sympathy for all subject peoples, can it remain detached from the demands for freedom made by articulate elements in the colonies (in form, part of Portugal) Angola and Mozambique, supported as these demands are by most of the independent African countries? Therefore the American government has tried to dodge the issue, reiterating its sympathy with the movement for independence, but trying to moderate the assaults on Portugal in and out of the United Nations Assembly. Will that moderating role continue to appease the Prime Minister who has governed Portugal so long and well, Antonio de Oliviero Salazar? In acknowledgment of Portugal's deep interest in preventing the spread of Communism, will he resign himself to the marginal influence exerted by American opinion on Portugal's troubles with its African colonies? Or will he refuse to prolong American use of the bases in the Azores unless the American government is completely inert? Or will he merely ask a larger financial premium? [4]

In short, the United States is blamed by African politicians for not coercing Portugal, by Salazar for coercing it, and opening the way not to democratic freedom in Africa but Communism. A third eventuality seems to me at least as real as either: chronic disorder, political instability, internal struggles and local wars.

Antipathies *between two or more* countries which the American

---

4. The bitterness of his remarks in the most serious speech on the subject delivered on August 12, 1963, is notable. In one passage he commented that ". . . the United States makes no secret of its African policy: great significance attaches to the official statements and to the facts of American administration designed to work for and to help with all its power [to] set up independent States all over Africa, corresponding to the former colonies or territories integrated in European nations. From this point of view, American and Russian policies may be looked upon as parallel and the fact that the United States aids the so-called emancipation of Africa to keep it free from Russian or communist influence makes little difference to the essence of things.

"Beyond this, however, there is a substantial difference: while Russian policy is coherent and logical, American policy involves a serious principle of contradiction. And it is this: while the fundamental principle of the policy of the United States is to help the defense of Europe, for which it has already made sacrifices in two great wars, it begins by provoking a reduction in the potential of its European allies in favor of the potential of its enemy, which is Communism." *The New York Times,* Aug. 13, 1963.

government is called on to assist may present similarly protracted dilemmas. They arise where it is not expedient to penalize either of the antagonists, since it is considered advisable to be helpful to both and use the chance afforded by friendship to try to reconcile them.

The American government, for example, is helping both India and Pakistan. But each glares at the other over Kashmir and each has kept its armies on the alert along their frontier. The resources they expend in maintaining military watch on each other offset or undo much of the benefit brought by American aid. Pakistan seems to be the more fearful and militant. Since the United States and Great Britain are providing India with enlarged amounts of military equipment and building up its air force to defend the frontier, the rulers of Pakistan have hinted that they might align themselves with Communist China if, in effect, the odds seem good. They seem to be trying to have the United States compel India to yield by threatening to cooperate with Communist China —perhaps in a new assault on India. Little wonder that some members of Congress now look with rue upon the billion dollars of American military aid and two billion of economic aid provided in years gone by.

Should the American government continue to shrug off the possibility and await events, or should it try to induce the rulers of Pakistan to be more temperate and to draw no closer to Communist China by providing the Pakistanis with more military equipment? Or should it reveal its resentment and suspend aid to Pakistan until its conduct and posture are more acceptable? At the end of August 1963 the American government plainly hinted it was on the verge of doing so; it objected to a contemplated civil aviation agreement between Pakistan and China and deferred a previously aranged loan for a new airport at Dacca, the capital of Pakistan.

The dilemma is the more vexatious because the American government is financing construction projects and health and educational programs in Afghanistan. But Pakistan and Afghanistan accuse each other of aggressive intent and their diplomatic and trading relations have been broken.

Longest lasting of all such dilemmas is due to the obdurate refusal of Arab states to abate their enmity to the state of Israel, and to discuss ways of resettling the Arab refugees from what used to be Palestine and the growing numbers of their progeny. For reasons of foreign policy the American government has been helping to build up both Israel and those states which are resolved to destroy it. Moreover, the United States is bearing a large part of the expense of maintaining a United Nations peace-watch, and of providing relief for the refugees. Meanwhile, one and all are using precious capital and foreign exchange—in part provided by us to aid their economies—to match or over-match the military forces of the other. Can this go on indefinitely? How far should it be permitted to go? Can no more incisive course be found than that being pursued by President Kennedy? Quizzed at a press conference about reports that German scientists and engineers were helping the United Arab Republic to develop a large missile force —potentially nuclear—he made the perplexed response, "We'll just have to wait and see what the balance of military power may be as time goes on. We are anxious to see it diminished rather than participate in encouraging it. On the other hand we would be reluctant to see a military balance of power in the Middle East which was such as to encourage aggression rather than discourage it. So this is a matter which we will have to continue to observe." [5] The dilemma is compounded by the fact that some of the assisted Arab countries conspire against others; the United Arab Republic against the regimes in Jordan and Saudi Arabia; and fitfully against the governments in office in Syria and Iraq (who knows who will be in office tomorrow?). Time is not likely to dissolve this dilemma. It is almost certain to come to a climax which will determine the future aid treatment of the protagonists.

In Southeast Asia the American government has been befriending the Philippines, Indonesia, and the former Malay States and

5. Press Conference—April 3, 1963.

Singapore. But after the latter two and other nearby former English colonial possessions were brought together in an independent Federation of Malaysia, the other two took this constructive development amiss. The government of the Philippines confined itself to mild expressions of displeasure. But the people and government of Indonesia acted almost as rabidly as the Chinese Communists. A mob in Jakarta raided destructively the Embassy of Malaysia and that of its ally, Great Britain. The Indonesian government stated that it was going to sever trade—which is of substantial dimensions —with and through Singapore. It took charge of British-owned plantations and other properties in Indonesia, disguising that act of vengeance as one of custodial responsibility. The patience of the American government, which has been due to excessive caution and concern for the situation of the American oil companies in Indonesia, broke at last. It announced that it would defer all further help to the Indonesian economy and for the program of stabilizing its currency. Quite correctly—though this may not have been the truly decisive thought—it explained that the actions being taken by Indonesia would condemn any currency stabilization program to failure, do severe damage to the Indonesian economy, and make the provision of further assistance futile. In my opinion this experience illustrates the chanciness of influencing the course and conduct of these remote regions of Southeast Asia by proffers of economic aid.

Within a decade American efforts to help the many needy independent African states may be tangled up in similar quarrels between them. The most important of the checkered situations in the central region as of now is caused by Ghana. The authorities of that country have been friendly to the West and beckoning to Communist supporters. It may try to impose its ideas and authority on smaller nearby countries which the Western democracies are helping. Yet the American government, in conjunction with American private enterprise, concluded that it was advisable to promise large sums to carry forward the construction of the Volta River dam, a huge project to supply electric power for industry, irrigation, for city and country. And to note another of conflict situations in Africa: the Somali Republic and Ethiopia, both recipients of our aid, are quarreling loudly and threatening each other.

In such situations our forked infusions of aid to both squabbling countries may turn out to have been wasteful or futile. Its inflow may actually make their quarrel more intense and dangerous. Yet, in general, I believe the American government has been wise to take the risks of aiding adversaries as long as there is a chance that their dispute may be kept under control and later resolved; to season its calming advice with constructive generosity. Though the peoples and governments of a country at odds with another are not as pleased as if the American government were helping them and refusing help to their adversary, each may be the more careful not to offend or seriously injure the United States, lest it then aid only the other.

Meanwhile the American government is trying hard to end the antagonism which provokes these dilemmas. It has been tireless in its efforts to conciliate Israel and its Arab enemies, offering to finance great projects of irrigation and power supply that would benefit them mutually. It has been persistent in its offers and attempts to act as mediator between India and Pakistan in their dispute over Kashmir. To that end in 1961, it proffered the services of Eugene Black, President of the International Bank; these were not used. A year later, Chinese Communist armies marched over the Himalayas into North India. When the Pakistan government complained because the American government hurried to aid the Indian forces, the American government sent Averell Harriman, then Assistant Secretary of the State for Far Eastern Affairs, to urge Ayub Khan and Nehru to reach an accord on Kashmir instead of persisting in their quarrel while the real enemy of both gloated. It has continued, without avail, to deploy its influence to bring about a resumption of discussions between the two governments. Similarly in the summer of 1964 Dean Acheson was sent to Geneva in order to assist the United Nations to devise an accord which might end the quarrel between Greece and Turkey over Cyprus.

When it cannot bring about a settlement of such disputes between recipients of aid, the American government worries along with them, hoping that in time they will fade away. As aptly summed up by Phillips Talbot, the Assistant Secretary of State for Near Eastern and South Asian Affairs:

> [The disputes between beneficiaries] are not only a source of continuing tension and a threat to the peace, but they also result in the dissipation of energies and resources badly needed for internal development . . . Accordingly, we are alert to every opportunity to help resolve these disputes. However, the countries involved are sovereign and there is a limit to what we can do to assist in the resolution of these conflicts. To attempt to deny all aid as a leverage to bring about solutions of largely intractable conflicts, would be impractical. Such an action might prove counter-productive and further limit any useful role which we can play in these conflicts. . . . In my opinion these disputes require the balm of time, patience and persuasion.[6]

In one other way the foreign aid program is caught in a cross-current of consequence that runs against the main charted course of foreign policy. This occurs when recipient countries enlarge their sales to Communist countries of strategic or industrially valuable goods. Stalin was convinced that the capitalist countries would sell to the Soviet Union the machines, materials and even industrial plants needed to hasten Soviet economic growth and increase its ability to manufacture military weapons. He based his conclusion on the Marxian premise that they would be driven to do so by the need to give employment and by the wish of capitalists for profit. Past and present events are proving that his expectations were in a measure correct. The Soviet Union and other Communist countries cannot get credits from the American government or from recipients of its aid. Nor can they directly get arms, or some of the machines or devices used only or mainly in production of weapons. But they have obtained, and are now ob-

6. Testimony, Subcommittee of Committee on Appropriations, House of Representatives, July 30, 1962.

taining, from some countries to whose productivity American aid has contributed greatly in the past, much else of value in sustaining Communism and strengthening the Communist military position.

It is almost needless to give examples. American private capital hurried along the development of the natural resources, industries and transport in Canada and Australia. These two countries have sold immense quantities of cereals to Communist China, making it easier for its rulers to keep down discontent and escape the consequence of their mistakes and dogmas. And Canada is providing the Soviet Union also with similarly great quantities of wheat. This will enable that country to avoid rationing of bread because of poor harvests and also supply the deficiencies of its satellites. Concern for the bank accounts of the farmers, brokers and shippers and for the finances of government agencies that hold the surpluses in these wheat-producing countries stilled uneasiness and colored vision, as it has at times in the United States. Those who benefit may don the guise of toleration and humanity and convince themselves that their remunerative activity is more likely to soften the spirits of sworn enemies than would punitive refusal.

In this hemisphere, Canada, Brazil and most other members of the Alliance for Progress continued to buy Cuban products and sell their products to Cuba until the Soviet long-range missiles were planted there. Castro's troubles were thereby eased and the despair which might have broken out in open rebellion was dampened. A Machiavellian mind might suspect that the reluctance of some Latin American governments to suspend trade and diplomatic relations with Cuba were touched by the thought that as long as Castro remains a dangerous threat, the United States will be more generous to them.

In the eighteen months before July 1961, the Communist bloc in Europe secured from the members of NATO about a billion dollars' worth of goods and equipment of strategic value for industry and military forces—products embodying new Western technology.[7] The German Federal Republic was the largest source of supply; Great Britain, France and Italy were the others. A quick glance down the list will show that it includes metal-fabricating plants, chemicals and electrical machinery, and plants for making them from Germany, large-gauge oil pipeline, pumping and refinery equipment from Germany, Italy and Japan—this the better to enable Russian oil to compete with Venezuelan and Middle Eastern oil in external markets, and deep sea oil tankers from the Western and Japanese shipbuilding yards. Some of the factories in which these and similar exports to the Communist bloc are made were financed in part by American private capital, and in a few American private capital has a dominant interest.

The British government has approved the export to Communist China of various kinds of machine tools, electric motors and generators, railway locomotives, internal combustion engines, scientific instruments and chemicals—all vital to China's development effort. Not long ago the Soviet government offered to place large construction orders for various kinds of ships to be built in British shipyards, which are now largely idle—to be paid for with Russian oil. Such a deal would hurt the oil exporting countries of the Middle East, North Africa and Venezuela and the large oil companies which operate therein and sell their production. The Conservative government turned down the proposition, but will a Socialist government? The answer may be given before the question is read.

Production and technology procured from his capitalist adversaries during the past decade made it possible for Khrushchev to boast, as he did to a group of visiting Japanese businessmen in August 1962: "The United States is in a state of lethargic sleep. . . . But though America does not trade with us, our rockets fly better than theirs. . . . This shows we can live without trade with the United States. . . . America produces good elec-

7. Sources: OEEC, *Foreign Trade, Overall Trade by Countries,* December 1960. See also Hearings, Oct. 23, 24, and 26, 1961, on Export of Strategic Materials to the U.S.S.R. and Other Soviet Bloc Countries before Subcommittee to Investigate the Administration of the Internal Security Laws of the Committee on the Judiciary, U.S. Senate, Parts 1, 2, 3, 4, and 6.

tronic machinery but again our rockets hit the targets more accurately than the American ones; and it is Soviet electronic equipment that was used in our missiles." [8] The Soviet orders for tankers, dredgers, oil pipelines and pumps, cranes, and electrical machinery now being filled by Japan and other capitalist countries that were aided by the United States, will help Khrushchev make good his boast. And Japanese industrial and commercial interests are avid to extend trade with Communist China.

The American government has fumed. But up to now in its efforts to persuade recipients of aid to curtail their trade with Communist countries—especially of strategic materials and products—it has had to rely on persuasion rather than threats. It has tried hard to make the officials and business interests of its allies pay more heed to the way in which our common enemies are being advantaged, and to cause them to realize that by allowing profit or economic necessity (depressed branches of industry and unemployment) to prevail over prudence they are endangering their own freedom and the lives of us all. Marx-Lenin-Stalin will be proven to have been correct.

However, both this political reasoning and American diplomatic influence may have even less effect in the future. For in the winter of 1963, lured by economic advantage and swayed by the wish to better relations with the Soviet Union, the American government approved large sales of cereals to Communist countries. Henceforth it will find it even harder to convince some of its allies that they should continue to restrict exports of strategic and vital products to Communist countries. For those of the allies who have endured hunger—such as Japan—regard food as the most vital import of all.

Unless trade with the Communist bloc is stiffly and selectively controlled, the Western capitalist countries will continue to get the worst of the bargain, as measured by basic economic and military benefits. For Communist governments can and do exercise such

8. *The New York Times,* Aug. 23, 1962, quoting from a report of Khrushchev's remarks given out by Tass, the Soviet news agency.

controls over their own exports; they do not sell products or processes or plants of pivotal value to their opponents. National advantage is their gauge; they sell primarily what they want most to sell, not what others want most to buy.[9] The free-enterprise countries in the main have been doing the opposite.

I would not want to seem to ignore the fact that some products procured from the Communist bloc in exchange—the lumber and metals, the machines and optical instruments, the equipment for dams, power plants, steel mills and fertilizer factories—have been of value to some struggling recipients, such as India and Egypt. Also, the Communist bloc, as buyers of their surpluses and suppliers of some products which they could not otherwise sell, may aid them. The resultant improvement in the general condition of such countries may in the long run lessen the appeal of Communism.

A similar scrutiny of the Soviet experience in foreign aid would conclude that it is beset by as many and as tough dilemmas as is the American program. Some would be the same in cause and kind; others would be different. I shall try briefly to point out a few.[10] My interpretation must be based largely on inference rather than on explicit public revelations. In the Soviet Union executive officials are not called upon to account openly for what they are doing, and where, how, why they succeeded or failed. There are no comprehensive volumes of Russian annual public hearings.

Of all the dilemmas which have harassed the Soviet govern-

---

9. The calculations guiding Communist control of foreign trade is well illustrated by statements in *The First Five-Year Plan for Development of the National Economy of the Peoples' Republic of China 1953–1957.* ". . . On condition that it benefits our socialist economic construction, we should continue to develop trade with other capitalist countries to increase imports of certain necessary materials.

"We should tighten the state's control over foreign trade to prevent capitalists from infringing our interests and to defend our socialist construction."

10. The dilemmas presented are clearly delineated in Donald S. Zagoria's book *The Sino-Soviet Conflict, 1956–1961,* to which I am much indebted for the historical information and interpretation in this section.

ment, the most serious ones are due to political mutability—the same kind of unexpected changes in alignment in the cold war which haunts the American aid program. Countries which it aided as allies have turned out to be unreliable, or may in the future turn out to be so.

The Soviet government helped Tito to restore the economic life of Yugoslavia after the war and get a good start on creating a dynamic Communist state. But Tito has not been willing meekly to conform to the wishes or example of Moscow, and Yugoslavia stands as a variant form of Communism to which other countries are attracted, despite Moscow's disapproval. Similarly, the Soviet government aided the newly independent Communist state of Albania to get under way. But that country and Yugoslavia are now living in a state of active hostility, and its rulers have defied Moscow and chosen to side with Communist China. This has caused the Soviet government to terminate its aid for Albania and to withdraw all Russian technicians from the country, and yet Albania remains as obdurate as before. Nasser is securing from the Soviet Union the tremendous dam and electric power at Aswan, as well as factories and processing plants. Yet the Soviet government sits by resignedly as he suppresses Communism in the United Arab Republic and shows a strong will to cling to his chances to consort with the West.

But these failures in the attempts to buy subservience have not counted or hurt as much as the blunt refusal of the Chinese government to stay in line with the originating center of international Communism. Here the mother's milk of Communism has soured; the Soviet government has suckled an ungrateful and accusing rival. When first the Chinese Communists gained control of their country, Stalin, having failed to foresee their victory, was indulgent toward their wishes and ideas. For a decade the Soviet government provided China's hustling regime with larger credits and grants and more varied technical aid and training than it did to all other countries. But after the 20th Congress of the Communist

Party of the Soviet Union, at which Khrushchev denounced Stalin, their views on ideology and aid tactics began to diverge, and the divergence became more tense and deep. The Chinese Communist leaders became openly critical of the Communist Party of the Soviet Union as revisionist. They remained so while the Soviet rulers in 1956–1957 were compelled to use force to quell unrest and rebellion in Poland, Hungary and Eastern Germany. And when Khrushchev gave help to these suppressed countries, to support their new rulers, the Chinese Communist leaders became openly disputatious. Yet, and possibly to secure their support against the European satellites, in October 1957 the Soviet government signed an agreement with the Peking government which stipulated that the Soviet Union was to provide China with a sample atomic bomb and technical information about the ways to manufacture them. During the next two years, as the Chinese continued to dispute Khrushchev's course and seemed to be striving harder for more influence in the international Communist world, he and his colleagues grew more angry and disturbed. They pondered the possible future impact of a disciplined, defiant, industrially-supported country of hundreds of millions of Oriental people crowding close against Soviet frontiers. Might not the intense hate Peking was spewing on the West at some later day be turned against Russia? Mao Tse-tung's dismissal of the consequences to the Soviet Union of a thermonuclear war against the West suggested the possibility.

Whether or not these were the determining thoughts, the Soviet government refused the Chinese Communist government the massive new credits wanted. And in June 1959 it abrogated the agreement to help Communist China be an atomic power; among the reasons given was that the cost would be too great for a people in such economic straits as were the Chinese people.

In an envenomed statement issued later by the Chinese Communist Party on the *ideological* origin and development of the differences between Moscow and Peking, the Chinese interpretation of this action was revealed. "The tearing up of the agreement on the new technology for national defense by the leadership of the C.P.S.U. and its issuance of the statement on the Sino-Indian border clash on the eve of Khrushchev's visit to the United States were presentation gifts to Eisenhower so as to curry favor with the U.S. imperialists and create the so-called 'spirit of Camp David.'" [11]

Gratitude for past help had by then turned into frantic resentment. Unwilling to lower their sights, the leaders of Communist China had imposed on the peasants the prison-like regime of "peoples' communes"; and their stimulators put millions of families and villages to making iron and steel in crude miniature furnaces set up in gardens and fields. Failure and trouble had not chastened the Chinese Communist leaders. They had become even more resistant and raucous critics of the Soviet government.

Angered by the Chinese tit-for-tat struggle in the meetings of the representatives of the many "fraternal" Communist parties, in July 1960 the Soviet government recalled all its technicians from China, and terminated all aid agreements.

Even those hurlers of epithets, those masters of accusation and insult among the early Bolsheviks might have felt they met their match in the composers of the diatribes being issued by the Chinese Communist Party at the present time. Two brief extracts from the statement already quoted will indicate how help may have hatred as its reward. "This whole train of events strikingly demonstrates that, disregarding everything, the leadership of the C.P.S.U. is allying itself with the imperialists, the reactionaries of all countries, and the renegade Tito clique in order to oppose fraternal Socialist countries and fraternal Marxist-Leninist parties," and "To put it plainly it is you [the Communist Party of the Soviet Union], and not we, who are defaming and discrediting the C.P.S.U. and the Soviet Union. Ever since the complete negation of Stalin at the 20th Congress of the C.P.S.U. you have committed innumerable foul deals. Not all the water in the Volga can wash

11.   The text of this long statement is in *The New York Times*, Sept. 14, 1963.

away the great shame you have brought upon the C.P.S.U. and upon the Soviet Union."

This short impressionistic account of Soviet experience with China is merely a reminder that the Soviet government has found economic aid as prankish a diplomatic instrument as has the American government. It must be aware by now that other countries which it is now helping may also leave its side. How can it be sure, for example, how East Germany will behave, if ever it gets the chance to break loose? Can it count on the faithful following of Indonesia? Or can it even be certain, despite the singular and costly Soviet effort to turn Cuba into a strong Communist base in the Western Hemisphere, that before "shrimps whistle" the Cuban people will not also throw off Communist rule? In sum, the Soviet government is taking as long chances as is the American government in its aid program.

The Soviet government also has in common with the American the dilemma posed by requests for aid by countries which are antagonistic to one another. China was not pleased by the aid given to India; or Pakistan by the aid given Afghanistan. I doubt whether the peoples and governments of Poland and Czechoslovakia are enthusiastic over the Soviet support of the industries of Eastern Germany. By concentrating its subsidies in the Western Hemisphere on Cuba, the Soviet Union has made most other Latin American countries aggrieved rather than envious. The compulsions of policy which have led the Soviet government, like the American, to help countries that dislike or are afraid of each other, have lessened the appreciation of each for the Soviet Union.

In the undeveloped and poor countries that have recently emerged or are emerging from a colonial status, the Soviet government faces an opposite dilemma from that of the American government. The aim of the Communist bloc is to bring about a Communist take-over of authority in these countries, either by the dissolution or deformation of the systems of government with which they entered into independence. To do so, they have to generate what Lenin called "a revolutionary situation."

This they have found a hard and baffling task. For in most of these countries the leaders of the nationalist, anti-imperialist independence movement were middle class. Their plans for progress are middle-of-the-road or a little left of the middle. Are they, the Soviet authorities must decide, to be given or refused economic aid? Should Communist governments support them, taking the risk that they will turn against factions sympathetic to Communism, when they are strong enough? So Lenin advocated before the Bolsheviks gained control of Russia; that they support all "Bourgeois-Democratic national liberation movements in countries under the influence of foreign capitalism even though they were not Communist and would not collaborate with the Communists"; a dictum since followed by the Soviet government more often than not.[12] Or should the Communist government take the other risk of losing the chance to advance the revolutionary process by penetration and association?

Whatever tactics they choose to follow, the Communist bloc must maintain the pose of benevolent friend to *all* newly founded nations and poor peoples. It must continue to seem eager to help them improve their lot. This, its spokesmen continue to profess they are willing to do merely because all are fellow travelers along the road to Socialist brotherhood. As exuberantly proclaimed, for example, a few years ago by A. A. Arzuman, the Soviet spokesman at the Afro-Asian Solidarity Conference in Cairo in 1957, "We are prepared to help you as brother helps brother, without motives. Tell us what you need and we will help you and send, according to our economic capabilities, money needed in the form of loans or aid . . . for industry, education, and hospitals . . ."

But action—the provision of Soviet economic aid—has lagged so far behind such professions as to indicate that the price is in reality

12. From an article written by Lenin in 1916 called "The Socialist Revolution and the Rights of Nations to Self-Determination," quoted in an article, "The National Democratic State," by William T. Shinn, Jr. in *World Politics*, April 1963, a most informative history of the argument over the tactics to be used in such situations in international Communist circles.

high. Moscow is supplying little except to countries and rulers on whom they can count.

Almost all nationalist-minded leaders in the newly independent and poor countries have been as reluctant—or more reluctant—to give Moscow conclusive pledges about their future political conduct as they have been to give them to the West. Although taking Communist help, few have been disposed to risk the loss of aid from the West. Some are using in reverse the same tactic to evoke Soviet generosity as that employed to get the Western democracies to bestir themselves; by hints or gestures to cause the Soviet government to worry over the possibility that, if left in distress, they might easily enroll in the Western political or military alliances.

Even the sporadic and limited aid which the Soviet government has found it expedient to give to countries or regimes which insist on remaining unaligned aroused the hostile criticism of the Chinese Communists. Khrushchev and his colleagues were compelled to defend their actions by Lenin's dictum that "the more backward the country . . . the more difficult it is for her to pass from the old capitalist relations to socialist relations." [13] But it is quite contrary to Mao Tse-tung's doctrinal declarations that revolutions may best be started among the ignorant and oppressed workers on the land, and can be carried forward merely by ruthless determination and agitation.

These brief comments on the dilemmas hedging and harassing the foreign aid activities of the Communist bloc are, I realize, only elementary treatment of a matter of major interest. Others, I know, are exploring it more thoroughly and more expertly.

13. See, for example, the explanatory defense made by O. Kuusinen, chief editor of the "Osnovy," otherwise known as "Osnovy-Marksizma Leninizma," 1959, at Lenin Anniversary Celebration in 1960. *Pravda*, April 3, 1960.

14 | Dilemmas Due to the Quirks of Economics

I turn to the dilemmas of decision that are encased in the *economics* of growth. Here again I shall only note a few of the more apposite.

Almost all that the poorer countries—except for a few densely crowded pockets like Hong Kong—have to sell abroad are foodstuffs, fibers, metals and other raw materials, unprocessed or processed. Each offers the foreign world its own assortment. Those who are large exporters of bauxite, iron ore, rubber and copper have not done badly. Sugar and tin exporting countries are at the present time gaining in income from exports of these products, but their advantage may be only temporary. The only ones who have done well constantly are those with great and low-cost oil deposits, the rising demand for which has thus far prevented the enormous potential supply from ruining the market.

Almost all the others have been hurt, in greater or less degree in common, by several trends—which sum up to one: the tendency for total supply of the main products they have to offer in international trade to increase more rapidly than the demand for them. The causes are diverse. Some industrial countries have imposed tariffs or quantitative restrictions on imports of various foodstuffs and raw materials to raise revenue, or to economize on foreign exchange, or to protect domestic producers. Some have become relatively more efficient and competitive producers of goods formerly bought from the poorer countries, being able to use more advanced methods of cultivation, and superior machines. Some, as their technology advanced, have also been economizing on use of natural materials, using less in the making of a product and/or substituting synthetics. Therefore their imports of the foodstuffs and raw materials exported by poor countries have not expanded as fast as their industrial growth. The effective demand of the poorer non-industrialized countries for each other's products has increased even more slowly. In contrast, the total world supply of these products has been distended. Native producers have been taught how to grow more on land already under cultivation and they have been helped to open up and plant other areas. Better methods of extracting and processing known sources of supply of raw materials have been introduced, and large hitherto unknown sources have been discovered and developed.

This situation has resulted in a relative depression in the prices received for many of the chief exports of the poorer countries since the bulge of prices caused by the war in Korea in the early nineteen fifties. Some have actually fallen, others have risen less than the prices of their main imports from industrialized countries. This has made it harder to earn by trade the amount of external purchasing power required to pay for the imports needed for development.

The diffusion of foreign capital and technical knowledge, the eagerness of every country to increase its exports, commercial competition—together—have done their work well. In some cases so well that the effects of foreign aid have been offset or cancelled.

In recent years the proceeds of the exports of the poorer countries as a whole have been about four times as much as all forms of foreign assistance received. Thus, should the relative retardation in the flow of their income secured from trade continue, it can be expected to incite more insistent demands for more foreign aid. For then, in the words used by the Finance Minister of Colombia, Jose Mejia Palacio at the meeting of the Governors of the Inter-American Development Bank in April, 1962 ". . . the help that is given . . . , however generous it may be will not be blood to vitalize our economies . . . but simply tranquillizers to avoid a total collapse."

The rage of producers of exports in the poorer countries and the frustration of their politicians and the social reformers who are trying to create better living conditions, may find vent in a sense of grievance against the more affluent countries akin to that felt by farmers in the American Middle West and South against the urban East when between 1880 and 1910 they were suffering a similar decline in their fortunes. But their William J. Bryan is more likely to talk and act like either Quadros, or Sukarno, or Khrushchev or Mao Tse-tung. They will excuse their failure to pull themselves out of difficulties through their own foresight and effort by placing the whole blame on the wealthier countries— which will not drink more coffee, tea, or cocoa; consume more sugar; eat more bananas; which use nylon instead of cotton, orlon instead of wool and furs, plastics and aluminum instead of copper, zinc, tin, and wood, synthetic chemicals, drugs, dyes, and industrial diamonds instead of natural ones.

To ease their lot and soothe their feelings, the American government may have to decide between three almost equally disagreeable alternatives: to make further grants and loans to tide over countries in distress caused by the lagging prices of their staple exports; or to assist them in arrangements for controlling the supply and prices of their products; or to acquiesce quietly if their governments restrict remittances of the earnings of American privately owned enterprises or purchases of American goods.

In the hope of rectifying the imbalance, most of the poorer countries are eager to diversify their economies by creating new domestic manufacturing industries, the product of which will replace imports. But few will be able to do so rapidly out of their own means and resources. Private foreign capital may be induced to start new industries by tariff protection and subsidies. But most of these poorer countries cannot make the inducement sufficient at the present time. Others do not care to confer favors on private foreign capital and so implant it firmly in their national life.

The further inflow of private foreign capital will lessen their difficulties if it either enlarges or diversifies the capacity of the poorer countries to export, or reduces their relative need for imports. If it does neither, the resultant financial pinch in the poorer countries will sooner or later become more painful. A larger fraction of the insufficient supply of foreign exchange will be wanted to remit earnings to the controlling foreign owners of local industries. Most oil and mining companies, unless prevented, will be able to take care of themselves by leaving abroad part of the proceeds of their own exports sold for dollars, pounds, marks, or francs. But the many other foreign-owned companies which sell to domestic buyers must either bid in the market for the foreign funds they want to remit or, where official control is exercised, apply to the authorities. In either case the strain on the balance of payments of the debtor countries may be intensified.

Another corrective proposed is the negotiation of international commodity agreements. In these only the producers of the product may join, or the chief importing countries may also participate in their operation. It may be agreed merely to restrict the amount of the product to be offered for sale in world markets by each of the exporting countries as a way of maintaining its price, or to set a range of prices within which the product may be sold and bought, or to do both. These agreements can work passably well if they are all-inclusive and if the prices maintained are not so much higher than costs of production as to induce still greater supplies from existing or from new sources. But one and all are likely to be vulnerable to the effects of advancing technology and the development of competitive products, natural or synthetic.

The American government, burdened as it is by the expense of supporting the prices of many domestic farm products, is justly unwilling to assume any direct financial obligation to support the prices of the exports of the poorer countries. However, it has ceased to oppose in principle accords that would maintain prices higher than those which would be procured in uncontrolled world markets. Thus, for example, the American government has encouraged and by its participation sanctioned an international agreement to control the volume of coffee offered on world markets and thus sustain its price.[1]

Countries which have deep deficits in their balance of payments because of events and circumstances they could neither foresee nor control, deserve sympathetic consideration. Those whose shortage of foreign funds is mainly due to their own faults do not.

The plight of some of the most pressing petitioners for aid in managing the deficits in their balance of payments is due to their careless compounding of unpaid debts to private foreign vendors. It is likely to be made worse by flight of domestic capital to escape the impact of rapid inflation or mistreatment. The responsible authorities may refuse to recognize or admit that these are the real causes of the troubling shortage of the means to pay abroad. Rejecting all critical analyses, they may maintain that their difficulties were unavoidable. Unrepentantly, they may confront the American government with a choice of bearing their ill-will, or

1. In the summer of 1964 representatives of the many countries that call themselves "undeveloped" met in Geneva to seek, by banding together, redress for their troubles. In the resolutions which they presented they claimed as their due not only greater financial aid and acceptance of plans that would support the prices paid them for their main exports, but also preferential trade treatment. This third proposal would, in my judgment, give rise to most troublesome discriminations. Behind the presentation of these and other claims there flickered the threat that in the event of refusal resentment might be given free rein and the temptation to align themselves with the Communists might prevail. To assure continuous attention to the plight of these countries a new permanent organization was created under the United Nations' auspices.

continuing to finance their laxity, or witnessing their default on debts to private or public lenders.

The responses of the American government cannot always be in accord with the rules of equity. It is sometimes even advisable to make up for an easily avoidable deficit in the balance of payments of some country. Such indulgence may be politically expedient. Or it may be an expression of belief that the lesson has been learned. Or it may be excused by the fact that only if the United States comes to the rescue, can or will the faltering country try to make the required reforms and innovations. However, as a general rule, the American government should be reserved toward appeals to finance deficits in the balance of payments that could have been averted or overcome by care and restraint. For if they are repeatedly reprieved, extravagant authorities will remain unconvinced of the need to adjust their desires and plans to their means. And foreign creditors, especially exporters, will be abetted in their inclination to over-sell and over-lend, either because most of the risk of loss is assumed by the American government—as many times it has been—or because of confidence that the American government will bail them out.

Let me single out the unavailing negotiations with the Brazilian government, which have dragged on these past four years, as an example of the difficulties of decision.

The political life of that country has been rent by division and wracked by irresponsibility. The rate of growth in production has been high. But the increase in national wealth and income was achieved by extreme fiscal and banking extravagance and it has left many millions in destitution. Though the American government and the international financial agencies had lent or given Brazil more than two billions of dollars during the past decade, its reserves of foreign exchange had been spent or pledged and current proceeds of its exports were barely enough to pay for essential imports. Thus it recurrently has been facing the prospect of defaulting on its foreign debts and restricting purchases of foreign goods required to continue various industrial projects and to alleviate misery in the vast northeast region.

The Brazilian government's most effective argument was, and is, that if it were not helped once again it might have to ration, control, or take over much private industry, and arrange larger barter deals with the Communist bloc. Would the United States want these possibilities to come to pass, the Brazilian government and press has asked when the American government and the international financial agencies seemed on the verge of refusing to come to the rescue unless the Brazilian government and people strove more earnestly to live within their means and end their financial chaos.

Extreme Brazilian nationalists warned their authorities not to compromise national sovereignty or dignity in return for aid. Wealthy conservatives cautioned against promises of tax and land reform which would disturb the traditional social system and stability. Government employees refused to defer demands for increases in their wages corresponding to the rise in the cost of living, as did the trade unions. The heads of Brazilian business feared that if the soaring inflation was stopped abruptly, they would be in trouble and be compelled to throw men and women out of work. Speculators in real estate forecast ruin for themselves and the banks from which they had borrowed. Leaders of peasant leagues and reformers insisted that projected schemes to alleviate misery of the many millions of extremely poor peoples in the northeast region—schemes vast enough to use up the whole savings of the country—must be pressed with utmost urgency.

The Communists and the labor officials and students who listen to them or consort with them did their utmost to exploit the situation. Brazil's woes, their claim is constantly made, were America's fault; Brazil's financial crisis was the time to cast out the imperialists, take over private industry and estates, turn to Socialism or Communism. The administration of President Goulart allowed the leaders of the Brazilian Communist Party to convene and agitate though the party is still illegal. Early in 1963 while the negotiations in Washington were still in an unsettled and abrasive state, Communist leaders from the world over—"fraternal delegates"—assembled in São Paulo for the most vociferous rally of years, to condemn us and praise Castro. Cynical observers wondered whether the Goulart government's esteem for civil liberties at this time was not sustained by the notion that such a spectacular expression of Communist activity in Brazil might affect responses to the requests of its Finance Minister who was then in Washington. Might not a specter scare the American government and the international financial agencies into relaxation of our terms after self-excusing persuasion had achieved all it could? Could not this be viewed as Brazil's way to have its foreign policy bring it foreign aid?

The agreement reached at that time, while tiding the Brazilian government over its straits, was intended to register the insistence of the American government that those who wished us to keep on providing means for economic growth must manage their own affairs satisfactorily. The measures which the Brazilian government promised to take would bring the economic life of the country into an orderly state and enable it to continue its economic rise, without the distortions and distresses which now disfigure it. The promised contribution of the American government and international agencies to enable Brazil to deal with its most pressing difficulties and provide support for key elements in Brazil's program for economic development was well advised and well reckoned.

But by the winter of 1963 Brazil's plight was as bad as ever. Inflation was going on as rapidly as ever and reaching the boundaries beyond which control would be impossible. The amount of paper money being printed to pay bills was greater than ever. The international value of the Brazilian currency was plunging further and further.

The Brazilian government was confronted by, and confronted the United States with a choice between going through a period of crisis with an unpredictable end, defaulting on its foreign obligations or securing more external aid.

Obviously this game of chance cannot go on indefinitely. At present, in 1964, after a great change in leadership, the Brazilian government at long last seems to be making a serious effort to begin to restore order in its economic and financial affairs and to regain the confidence of foreign suppliers of aid. Brazil's foreign creditors are giving it more time to make its actions match its avowals.

The problem of decision encountered in this instance indicates how the administrators of aid must and can combine deference to the exigencies of international politics with an effort to serve the professed purpose of aid—economic and social betterment.

Another set of policy dilemmas arises from the difficulty of knowing in advance how best to evoke the desired political response to American aid. These should perhaps be called working perplexities rather than policy dilemmas. Though I cannot adequately explain the complexities of the two I have in mind nor set down any guiding principles sufficiently precise to be useful, I cannot abstain from pointing them out again, for I have already touched on both.

The first is the problem of adjusting the wish that recipients of American aid accumulate the capital needed for sustained economic growth to the wish to avoid extremes of economic and social inequality. The other is the problem of adjusting the wish to increase the total product of recipients to the wish that all who want work and are able to work can have the chance to work.

Neither of the dual aims involved in these two areas can be relinquished, or too greatly subordinated to the other. Priorities should always be provisional and flexible. All that can be said with positiveness, I think, is first that governments should hurry along the accumulation of capital as fast and to as great an extent as their people will voluntarily bear the necessary restraints and impositions. However, they need not countenance exceedingly great inequalities of income—between the very few at top and the very many at bottom. Losses in productivity due to relatively slow rate of capital accumulation can be more than made up by the increase in the production of the working millions if they can procure more and healthier food, medical care, housing and education. Second, governments should favor fields and forms of activity that provide useful work for the great number of idle or half-idle people rather than concentrate on the creation of highly automated huge-scale industries, even those which produce capital goods.

In its own national affairs the United States has found it hard to keep a good balance between these alternative ends of government activity. It has had to change course frequently to equilibrate; and it can hardly expect to do otherwise in directing the foreign aid policy. Obviously there is no single or simple formula of decision for all recipients or even for any one country at all times and under all conditions. Aid administrators will have to ask themselves anew every time they turn a page on the calendar: which proportional distribution of our aid to any country is likely to produce the healthiest local situation and healthiest relationship between the United States and the recipient?

When driven to distraction, they may derive some comfort from two general observations about past experience. In the long run as capital has become more abundant, democracies have found it easier to reconcile progress and equality. And in the long run total productivity and total employment are likely to rise and fall together. But many local officials will be indifferent to and unwilling to trust to these slowly operative tendencies. Abstract economic theories that command credence in the United States flutter in the winds of doubt and fade out in the quite different atmosphere of very poor countries.

15 | National or Multinational Action

Can international agencies deal more easily than national ones with the obstacles and dilemmas encountered? Could such agencies serve the main and permanent aims of foreign aid as well or better than national governmental bodies?

Even in summary examination of these questions, significant differences will appear in the acceptability and value for different tasks and purposes between 1) "universal" international agencies like the United Nations, which include almost all independent states including those that are Communist, and 2) "multinational" agencies—like the International Bank for Reconstruction and Development—a smaller company without Communist elements and 3) regional agencies such as the Colombo Plan, the Inter-American Bank and the Alliance for Progress.

Perhaps as good a way as any to approach the subject will be to follow the trail of the conceived advantages of purveying American aid through international agencies made by Assistant Secretary of State Harlan Cleveland, in support of the appropriations for the Foreign Assistance Act of 1961.[1]

1. Hearings, Subcommittee of the Committee on Appropriations, House of Representatives, August 16, 1961.

First, "the use of international agencies for the maintenance of peace and order can avoid competitive intervention by rival nations on the Spanish Civil War model. The United Nations can be brought in without being accused of intervention to keep order and build up the machinery of government in a new nation—because U.N. action is taken in the name of the world community; because it is clearly in the interests of peace; and because its motivation is beyond suspicion or national or commercial ambition. This is the case of the United Nations Emergency Force in the Middle East, and more recently, the United Nations Operation in the Congo."

International agencies are of singular usefulness in such special assignments as these, and for the reasons given. However, the United Nations can function as envisioned only if, and in so far as, the opposed combinations of powers which exist within it *all* prefer temporary calming of a situation to a test of their opposed influence and dangerous local war or disorder. Then the services of the UN—supplanting rivalries—may be invaluable for peace and most helpful for the countries which become international wards.

Second, "Some of the newly emerging nations are understandably sensitive about accepting technical conditions for assistance from one of the great powers. . . . This sensitivity is eliminated or greatly reduced when the aid is furnished through an international organization of which they are members and from which they are willing to accept conditions for aid. . . . The same advantage of working through international organizations also carries into some kind of preinvestment activities where a single nation might be suspected of seeking to shape another's development program for selfish ends. In short, in some of the politically sensitive countries an international agency can lay down stricter conditions for aid than a single country."

The same opinion was more positively affirmed by Eugene Black in his Farewell Address to the Board of Governors of the IBRD—which is a multinational but not all-embracing international institution—in September 1962.

Foreign Aid and Foreign Policy | 216

> An international organization will make aid available with the
> sole purpose of helping the country receiving that aid. . . . Be-
> cause they are known to have no ulterior motive, they can exert
> more influence over the use of a loan than is possible for a bi-
> lateral lender: they can insist that the projects for which they
> lend are established on a sound basis, and—most important—they
> can make their lending conditional on commensurate efforts being
> made by the recipient country itself.

This has been so in some situations, and it may be so in many
others. Refusal by a national supplier to finance a locally favored
project because it is not justified may be construed as a wish to
protect a foreign interest or as a mark of opposition to the government making the request. A turn-down by an international organization may not arouse the same suspicion and rancor.

Officials, afraid of losing power if they end extravagant financial
policies, may regard as a rude rebuff the refusal of a foreign national contributor to provide new means for paying off old debts,
and may so portray it to the populace. A multinational organization may be able to preach the virtues of sobriety and solvency
and insist on their observance without drawing a direct shaft of
reproof on itself. Even if the displeasure is not dispelled, it may
be buffered as was that of the Argentine and Brazilian authorities
in 1963, at the obduracy of the International Monetary Fund
in requiring fiscal responsibility before salvaging their financial
situations.

Insistence by foreign national officials that a petitioning country must qualify itself for aid by reforms—economic, fiscal, social,
administrative, legal—may be resented as use of money power to
dominate, even though the need for reform is indisputable. The
same petitioner may, however, think it can yield with more dignity to the same stipulations when made under international auspices. Similarly, conditions of self-help that would be rejected as
too onerous if proposed by a national supplier may be acceptable
if proposed by a multinational agency—especially one in which
needy countries are active and respected members.

In these ways, multinational aid-agencies may now and again be able to perform better than national ones. However, in regard to any all-embracing international agency such as the United Nations, these advantages remain hypothetical rather than proven. For all members formally have equal standing and an equal right to be helped. The division of its funds between the many claimants is affected by their politics within the organization. Favors are exchanged. Opposition is matched by opposition. Decisions may reflect mutual accommodation rather than willingness to conform to the requirements of effective use of aid conferred.

> Third, "International agencies offer one important device for raising the contributions of other nations which can afford to help."

That is so. But up to the present, the universal organizations have failed to elicit large supplementary contributions from their members. Neutrality does not evoke generosity. However, the more limited multinational agencies have been able to induce some countries to make what is for them substantial contributions to the common fund because of the better chance they have to play a genuine part in managing this fund and of drawing upon it.

> Fourth, "The international agencies can draw on a world-wide pool of technical personnel which may not be available in the United States. In many cases, non-American technicians have experience which is more relevant to conditions obtaining in the less developed world. Moreover, internationally sponsored technical assistance can often be purchased at lower cost if non-American technicians are involved."

The training and experience of foreign technicians in many matters may make them better qualified than available Americans; the Danes in modern dairying for example; the Norwegians in maritime work and fishing; the French in general education; the Israelis in dry land farming and agricultural cooperation; the Japanese in light industries using much labor and little machinery of the more massive kinds; the British in government administration.[2] Certainly the expert knowledge of all should be summoned to help. In some countries or situations the presence of numerous American technicians arouses dislike or suspicion. A group of technicians from many countries may be more cordially treated. Their joint advice and instruction may be more trustfully considered. In other countries or situations, the American technicians and advisers may be more welcome and trusted than those of any other nationality.

However, the business of selecting these agents of aid from the wide world and welding them into an efficient and harmonious working group is not easy. Operating in different languages is an extra strain on all. Differing national tastes, customs and standards of performance have to be accommodated. Clashes of personal temperaments or ambitions may be aggravated by national attachments.

Also, weight should be attached to the likelihood that American technicians will be more mindful of American interests and purposes than those of other nationalities, if only because they are in more continuous and closer contact with American life and ideas. Most of them will be more intent on making friends for the United States than would hired foreign technicians, and more on guard against any attempts to use American aid to benefit opponents of the West.

> Fifth, "International agencies are better equipped to help in regional projects overlapping national boundaries."

This may be so. But it will be so only when there is harmonious accord within the agency. If split into factions, as is the United Nations, it may not be able to undertake regional projects of recognized merit; or if it does so, it may not be able to carry them out capably and expeditiously.

2. These are only some of the fields in which technicians of one or another country may surpass those of others mentioned in Robert Asher's interesting article, "Multilateral Versus Bilateral Aid," in *International Organization,* Autumn 1962.

Sixth, "The healthy growth of international agencies is in itself an important U.S. objective. Multilateral organizations, endowed with capacity to act in the interest of security and development, can promote the open world society of independent and prosperous nations which is the goal of our foreign policy—and which stands at the opposite extreme from Soviet dreams of a Communist one world."

Here Harlan Cleveland's exposition soared into political space where obscure language is easily mistaken for precise analysis. Of course, multinational agencies *can* promote a world society of the kind for which the American people long. But *will* they, if the preponderant disposition of its members is toward the Communist line rather than that of the Western capitalist countries, or indifferently cool to both?

All these contingent advantages of using the United Nations (and other all-embracing international agencies), even if realized, would not relieve the American government of the need to watch whether by reason of the disposition of the majority of the members, that organization is sufficiently mindful of American interests in the cold war; mindful on balance, on clear balance, though not in every matter or issue.

Even if the international agency passes that test, only a fraction of American aid activities should advisedly be put under its custody at present. For no international agency of this sort could or would assure that the dispensation of our contribution was in close conformity with American foreign policy. Its general rule would almost certainly be subject to that principle which was enunciated by the General Assembly of the United Nations in 1948 in a resolution supporting an enlarged program of technical assistance; that the activities of the United Nations in this field shall "Not be a means of foreign economic interference in the country concerned and shall not be accompanied by any considerations of a political nature." Thus it could not adjust priorities among the recipients to their internal political or social characteristics or to their behavior in international affairs. It could not—as can the American government when the issue or situation is important enough—adjust its treatment of individual applicants for aid according to its stand in the struggle against Communism or other disturbing issues.

The import of these general considerations may be clarified and enhanced by a summary review of the past performance of the main multinational agencies which have engaged in the provision and management of aid—of capital and technical assistance—to the poor and undeveloped countries.

To look back to that first international agency which was expected by its founders to lead in cooperative conduct of these activities—the League of Nations. It was cramped from the start by the impoverishment of its main European members, maimed by the absence of the United States, and harassed by the rise first of Bolshevism, then of Fascism. Thus its economic and financial activities did not thrive and expand as the originators hoped. Despite the devoted efforts of a talented staff, the successes of the League in aid of its poorer members were few. The most notable were the international loans it sponsored during the nineteen-twenties for Austria, Hungary and Greece, which enabled these countries to master emergencies and make a start toward orderly recovery. The League also helped to arrange consortiums of private investment bankers of the former allied and associated nations to make loans to Germany. Thereby it temporarily eased friction over reparations, enabled Germany to regain currency stability, and facilitated its economic recovery. But these contributions toward the betterment of the international scene were lost during the decade of the thirties, as the depression deepened and Hitler and Mussolini strode ahead. The League, deserted by some of the larger countries, ignored by others, lost vitality. It became merely a gathering place for those few devoted diplomats who clung to its ideals and forms. Its economic activities froze in the cold international winds.

At the end of the Second World War, the creators of the United

Nations hoped the nations had learned the need and blessings of living and working together in peace. Within its fold an Economic and Social Council was formed, as a prospective complement of the Security Council, to guide or supervise the many specialized United Nations sub-agencies or affiliates that were to engage in cooperative economic and social activities.[3]

Since it would be far beyond my reach in space and knowledge to recount and analyze the manifold activities of these agencies and affiliates, I must leave the reader to learn as much as he wants to know from the thousands of pages of available reports and studies.

Summarily, their efforts, though probably too diffused and often too little or transient, have been, by and large, useful and inspiring. They have benefited in some way and measure many poor and miserable people.[4] They have held a great humanitarian

3. These are:

> Special United Nations Fund for Economic Development (SUN-
> FED)
> United Nations Bureau of Technical Assistance Operation (BTAO)
> Food and Agriculture Organization (FAO)
> United Nations Educational, Scientific and Cultural Organization
> (UNESCO)
> World Health Organization (WHO)
> International Labor Organization (ILO)
> International Civil Aviation Organization (ICAO)
> International Telecommunication Union (ITU)
> World Meteorological Organization (WMO)
> International Atomic Energy Agency (IAEA)
> United Nations International Children's Emergency Fund (UNI-
> CEF)
> United Nations Special Projects Fund (UNSPF)

4. The variety of their activities is astounding, and quite probably too scattered to be fully effective. This may be illustrated by listing those fields in which just one of these agencies—the Bureau of Technical Assistance—has been engaged or is now engaged in India alone:

Agriculture education, extension research, economics and statistics
Antibiotics and insecticides
Chemical engineering
Coal and metal mining
Crop production and protection
Dairy development
Electronics
Engineering (civil, mechanical, structural highways, etc.)
Fertilizer survey
Forestry and forest industries
Fisheries development
Glass molds

purpose above the lashing and damaging storms of international politics. Yet, in total, their achievements after almost twenty years have been far less than the founders of the United Nations had hoped they might be.

The tasks set for these aid-agencies of the United Nations in any case would have been rigorous. But the effort to perform them has been constrained by the same adverse circumstances that have crippled the political activities of the parents of the organization. Some of its wealthier members have not been willing to put larger sums for economic aid at its disposal because of their outlays for military purposes. Others (or the same) suffered losses of income from their foreign investments in former colonies which threw off their guardianship.

Most stunting of all has been the conflict with Communism which has divided two sets of its members, inside and outside of the United Nations conference rooms. This has caused the largest potential contributors to give much less than they would have otherwise. It has made them unwilling to assign to the United Nations a primary part in the distribution of aid except in such otherwise unmanageable situations as have been noted. They have clung to the influence which the power to grant or deny aid may give them; to reward or punish, or treat with unconcern; to choose to give help without any stipulations or attach stipulations that are implicit and vague or explicit and taut. Despite this fact, the capitalist countries, especially the United States, have given much the largest share of the funds of the United Nations agencies.

Hydro-electric transmission
Labor administration
Leather technology
Manufacture of sulfuric acid
Maternity and child welfare
Medical and health education
Nursing education
Pencil manufacturing
Petroleum geology
Photogrammetry
Population studies

Ports and shipping
Preventive and social medicine
Productivity studies
Re-insurance
Rural electrification and rural welfare
Sheep and wool
Statistics
Steel foundry techniques
Soil engineering and soil conservation
TB control
Vocational guidance

This rift has hampered the benevolent activities of the United Nations in still other ways. The capitalist members have usually been well disposed toward plans and projects that might bring about an expansion of private capital and enterprise; the Communist members have tried to persuade the poorer countries to debar private capital and extend government ownership and control. The capitalist members are more interested in providing those kinds of technical aid that will enable small-scale, private, peasant farming to prosper; the Communist members do not wish to have this class enlarged and strengthened. The Western democracies have been receptive to initiatives that would let supporters of constitutional government climb into office and stay there; the Communist states have done what they could to check them. The thoughts and the aims of the one set have centered on orderly economic progress and social reform; those of the other set have centered on chaos and revolution.

Internal tensions have also made it harder to correct faults and detect failures in the operations of these agencies. In selecting officials, both for permanent posts and temporary assignments, national affiliation and political philosophy have sometimes brought in inferior men and passed over better ones; and once in office all but the few top officials are protected from criticism. Their work, being covered by the glaze of international cooperation, has escaped inspection as thorough as that to which national programs are subjected. There has been some wasteful competition and duplication of effort between the several subordinate or affiliated agencies. Each has its own sprawling ambitions, its busy staff eager for promotion, its own ideas of duty and aims of achievement. Its members (except the Soviet Union and France) have been lenient to these imperfections lest by harsh criticism they weaken the main structure of the United Nations. They have kept their mouths shut and their purse strings tight.

For all these reasons, the United Nations has not yet managed to work out a coherent rationale—economic, political, and social—through which its effort in aid could be culled, shaped, and merged into an effective unity. To belie these faults by evangelical appeals is futile. To cease to try to eliminate them would be regrettable.

More than half the members of the United Nations need the much greater assistance which conceivably could be arranged and conducted through its agencies. Let them reflect more intensely on the causes which have cramped its efforts and achievements.

The International Bank for Reconstruction and Development was conceived as a universal organization. But the Soviet government and its satellites refused to join. Their absence, which makes decision much simpler and its operation much smoother, has lessened its chance to act as mediator between the capitalist West and the Communist countries.

The designated tasks of the Bank are:

> . . . to assist in reconstruction and development by facilitating the investment of capital for productive purposes . . . to promote private foreign investment by means of guarantees or participations in loans and other investments made by private investors; and when private capital is not available on reasonable terms to supplement private investment by providing finances for productive purposes out of its own capital, funds raised by it and other resources.[5]

Since relative voting power is proportionate to the size of national capital subscriptions, the Western capitalist countries are able, when they wish, to control the Bank's activities.

During the first post-war years when the financial position of most countries was parlous, its directors were prudent. The Bank preserved its capital, while wooing the esteem and trust of the treasuries and financial institutions of the main members. In accordance with its constitution it has required payment of interest and repayment of principal on its loans on terms akin to—although less onerous than—those that would have been asked by private

5. Bretton Woods Agreement, 1944.

financial groups. It stepped aside whenever such groups were willing to offer the needed capital "on reasonable terms." Thereby it created a firm image of itself as a bank, not a benevolent institution; a bank trying to supplement rather than supersede the activities of private capital.

As a rule the heads of the Bank have been allowed to choose the staff on the basis of professional qualification. National member governments have observed similar standards in appointing their representatives on the Board of Governors. Up to now all presidents have been Americans—*primus inter pares.*

As the Bank grew stronger and richer it financed more and more originative works on all continents. Member governments have readily subscribed to additions to its capital. Private financial houses have bought large amounts of its bonds which are good investments. Private bankers have come to know its management and personnel and are familiar with its methods of doing business.

Eager but not over-eager, adroit but not deceitful, its history has been smooth. It has done much to create in many countries what has become known as the "infra-structure" of a diversified and fecund economy, the essential bases for more efficient agricultural and industrial production; as for the dredging, improvement, and equipment of ports, the building of roads and railroads, the installation of irrigation and drainage works, the control of water power and its conversion into electric energy, the construction of steam and even atomic power plants, the provision of adequate municipal water supplies. It has also loaned money for plants to manufacture fertilizer, cement and paper, to preserve and process foods, to tan hides, to refine sugar and oil. It has also assisted various countries to develop public and private banking and credit institutions. With few exceptions the projects it has supported have been well conceived.

In short the Bank has earned its good repute. It has done much to make it easier for poorer countries to start forward, acting in this as a valuable adjunct to, and steward of, the national efforts of the Western capitalist countries. Its record indicates the advantages which may be had by channeling aid through a multi-national agency, when that agency is not hampered by deeply internal divisions and not hard driven by political considerations.

However, the nature of its designated tasks made it easier for the Bank than for any other multinational agency to avoid mistakes, losses and angry complaints. It has not been required to salvage desperate financial situations. It has seldom been pressed by its more influential members to finance an unsound undertaking because it was diplomatically desirable. Thus it has been comparatively free to select its ventures according to their intrinsic value to the countries in which they were carried out. It has been able to make such stipulations as it thought fit to assure that its loans would be well used. It has usually been permitted to exercise supervision over the progress of the projects it financed. It has not been expected, as is the United Nations, to heal the deep gashes in the world it assists.

Even so, and despite the excellence of its management, the Bank would have had a much more troubled course had not the American and other governments eased its way, and saved it from disputes over payment on some of its loans. They—particularly the American government—took over the burden of providing means for projects and purposes that could not be converted into bankable operations, and those which were too politically touchy. Time and again, by coming to the rescue of the debtors, they spared the Bank the annoying necessity to act as hard-faced banker, demanding payment on its loans from governments in financial distress. The American (and other) Treasuries have in these and other ways given continuous shelter to both the borrowers from the Bank and the Bank.

Recently the Bank has begun to move into shakier and rougher territory. Impressed by the need, the members of the International Bank agreed in 1960 that its operations should be expanded into areas of productive promise that could not currently pay for themselves. For this purpose they established an affiliated institution, the International Development Association known as IDA. This is expected to be as thorough as the Bank in preparation and supervision of the projects it sponsors. But it is authorized to finance initiatory works of development on far easier and more flexible terms. The credits which it has been extending are repayable over a period as long as 50 years, starting only after the first 10 years, and virtually without interest. Thus, they are almost as light on the recipients as grants would be. Yet they contain a reminder that debtors had better manage their affairs well since ultimate repayment is expected.

The experience of the International Development Association has been so brief that comments on its prospects must be conjectural. If the international situation does not deteriorate further, the scope and volume of its activities will expand rapidly. For more of the needier nations will have reached—as some have already reached—the limits of their capacity to pay interest, in convertible funds, on the usual terms asked by institutions run by national governments to finance their foreign trade (in the U.S. the Export-Import Bank) and by the International Bank, and also to allow private foreign investors to remit their earnings home. The foreign obligations of most of the poor countries in great need of capital have mounted more rapidly than their export earnings. Hence, as correctly and tersely concluded by Eugene Black, "If the momentum of development is to be maintained, it can only be by grants or loans at very long term and at very low interest."

IDA will not be able to get along with as little international hubbub as the International Bank. Some of its most eager clients are in political disorder, and some are in financial and economic distress as well. But IDA is not supposed to hold itself aloof, as can the Bank, and avoid the more disturbed situations and select the safer ones. It was formed to treat with countries in trouble and to finance risky ventures; by so doing to use its limited means to quiet or transform the weaker societies.

Given half a chance and more capital, I anticipate that IDA will justify the faith which led to its creation. It has the authority and can command the experience. It may be able to operate in some of the poorer countries more effectively than could the American government alone. As has been remarked, the pride or resentment of some of these peoples tends at times to surpass their reason. Then American awards are exposed to the darts of suspicion, imputations of hidden purposes, racial and national prejudices, and enemy propaganda. But IDA will not be immune from mistrust and unfair fault-finding. It, too, will be regarded by some as stern and scheming, since its sponsors have directed its managers, when considering requests for low-cost loans, to take into account the alacrity of petitioners to respond to advice that they do more to help themselves and make essential reforms.

The International Bank and the International Development Association have joined with national governments to finance a few basic development projects which required great sums of capital. Each of the participants thereby lessened the call on its resources and the risks. Their combined professional talent is being made available for the better planning and execution of the projects supported. By such conjunction of multinational and national sponsorship the hesitations of both the contributors and the beneficiaries may be overcome. The national participants can be a little more assured that their wishes will not be disregarded than they could be if the auspices of the project were wholly multinational. The beneficiaries are, on the other hand, well insulated against unfair national pressures; they may therefore be less resistant to stipulations laid down to assure honesty and efficiency.

Two main examples of this type of joint undertaking between the IBRD-IDA and national governments indicate the possibilities. One is the Volta River hydro-electric project in Ghana. The total anticipated cost for the dam, the power plant, and the transmission grid is 196 million dollars. Of this the American government is contributing 37 millions, the British government 14 millions, the International Bank 47 millions, the government of Ghana the remainder. It may be surmised that this combination was, in part, encouraged by the hope that the government of Ghana, which has been inclined to associate closely with the Communist group, would respond better than if the venture were financed solely by the Western governments; and that, on the other hand, the American Congress would not put up either the whole amount required, or even approve a large participation in the project unless the American government was able to hold up the development if Ghana's treatment of the United States should become intolerable. The other example is the consortiums formed to assist Pakistan and India in their burgeoning national plans. At the time of writing, of the total of about 1.2 billions of dollars to be set aside for Pakistan, the American government is obligated to contribute about half, the IBRD-IDA about a quarter, and the other countries (the United Kingdom, France, Germany, Japan and Canada) the other quarter. In India the total sum visualized is over 2 billions, and of this again the American government is obligated to contribute almost half, IBRD-IDA about 20 per cent, and other contributing countries, including Austria, Belgium and the Netherlands, the remainder.

Besides entering into joint ventures with multinational agencies, the main non-Communist suppliers of aid have begun to concert and coordinate the flow of their grants and loans to the poorer countries as well as the investments of their nationals therein. This is the assignment of the Development Assistance Committee (DAC) of the Organization for Economic Cooperation and Development (OECD). In this group the American government comes together with various European associates, Canada and Japan.

In 1961 all approved a recommendation that "members agree to expand the flow of resources to the less-developed countries, to improve the effectiveness of development assistance, and to provide for increased assistance in the form of grants or loans on favorable terms."

If these main suppliers do coordinate and concert their actions the whole efflux of assistance can be made more generative and equitable. The chance that the short-term repayment obligations that one or another supplier may impose upon a postulant will obstruct more productive longer-term programs of aid contemplated by another will be lessened. Rivalries between the countries associated in DAG, all standing out against Communism, can be averted or adjusted. By presenting themselves as a unified group with a great common purpose rather than as competitors with self-centered national aims they will make a better impression and elicit a better response.

Governments that seek help but are unwilling or unable to do what ought to be done to deserve it, will find it harder to extract aid by haggling. Relative responsibilities can be designated for assisting countries or regions toward which any one or several of the suppliers has a special interest relation—as has the United States toward Latin America, France and Belgium toward their former colonies in Africa, Great Britain toward its former colonies and present dependencies, Canada perhaps toward the West Indies. In these and other ways a common front in the extension of aid may not only add to the effectiveness of the aid but may make the opposition to Communism less fracturable.

The American government has been the prodding member of the Development Assistance Committee. To reduce its own outlay for foreign aid it is now trying to persuade its associates, since they are prospering again, to do more on easier terms. As has been previously commented on, their loans, grants and investments have been growing rapidly. But American official opinion that they ought to be doing still more has become sharp and its expression has become more open. This is indicated in the passage in the Clay Committee report that stated:

> We are convinced that the burden of sustaining foreign assistance to the less developed countries is falling unfairly on the United States and that the industrialized countries can and should do more than they are now doing. The present inequity is even more apparent when one adds defense expenditures to economic assistance to determine the national shares in the total expense of protecting and advancing free world well-being.

President Kennedy echoed this opinion in his subsequent message to Congress. Congress endorsed it. However, it is not proving to be easy for the United States to arouse its associates to show enthusiasm for aiding the poorer countries equal to its own, and to take the lead in the attempt to bring about world-wide material improvement while the United States temporarily pauses.

Akin to the DAC but more restricted in membership and scope are the Development Fund and Investment Bank of the European Economic Community. Their original six-member governments have contributed, up to the time of writing, about 600 million dollars. Grants are being made for economic and social projects which could not be self-supporting in the former colonies of the members of this group and associated members of the Common Market, such as Turkey. By augmenting their supply of food and raw materials, by helping them modernize and diversify their economic activities, the Fund may ease slightly the task of the political leaders who are being initiated into the ways and trials of self-government. But the period of operation of this Fund has been short and is terminable, so that judgment about the value of its performance must rest in suspense.

Similar to IDA, but regional in its membership and sphere of activity, is the Inter-American Development Bank (IDB). In this the United States joins with the other members of the Organization of American States to stimulate economic growth and social progress in the Western hemisphere. Its policy and practices are linked with those of the Alliance for Progress.

The IDB is authorized to carry out three quite different kinds of transactions. Out of its own capital funds it makes loans on terms and conditions that approximate banking practice. Since all loans from this source must be approved by a two-thirds vote, and since the voting weight of each member is proportionate to its capital contribution, the American government can, when it wishes, exercise final say. Out of more than a half-billion dollar

Social Progress Trust Fund donated by the American government but administered by this Bank, many loans are being made on such "soft" terms as to be really grants for schools, medical and public health centers, land reform, low-cost housing, and similar institutions and activities. Over the decisions of this Fund the American government has less control. Congressional committees have recently expressed the belief that the Bank was not being rigorous enough in insisting that beneficiaries of the Fund do all they can to effect reforms and make the effort necessary to achieve social progress. Thirdly, out of a Fund for Special Operations, also entrusted to the Bank, loans repayable in whole or in part in the currency of the borrower are arranged.

The officials and the people of the Latin American countries may be more at ease in dealing with an organization of which they are responsible partners—an organization which belongs to them and is largely run by them—than with a single national government. Most of them may take a more serious view of their obligations to such an institution and be more responsive to its requirements and more eager to meet its expectations. But some are testing the chances of using their place within the Bank to bargain for unmerited help on inferior projects. Loose spenders are trying to draw on the combined funds to avoid the necessity of living more nearly within their means.

The primary test of the value of this Inter-American Bank—as of the Alliance for Progress with which it is linked—will be whether it can induce its more faltering members to do what they must to make its help lastingly useful. Will they in company adopt good common standards of qualification for aid and live up to them? Or will most of its members be lax in their requirements, each being fearful lest it, in turn, may be asked to give pledges or subscribe to plans that call for unwelcome austerity or reforms which chafe or mortify?

Different from any of these international agencies is the Colombo Plan for Cooperative Economic Development in South and

Southeast Asia. This is a grouping of sixteen countries in that region and six outside (Australia, New Zealand, Canada, Great Britain, the United States and Japan). The organization acts as a connective agency and clearinghouse, not as an administrator. It has no capital of its own to dispense and no authority to levy on its members. But they are obligated to help each other the better to plan development programs and to secure the requisite capital and technical assistance. In the meetings of representatives of its members, the poor ones can get serious attention for their needs. The staff assists in the preparation of their requests and in the working out of helpful arrangements. The sums which the more wealthy members have provided to carry out programs and projects worked out in consultation have been substantial.

Through its convocations an atmosphere has been created in which all, the more and the less developed, the richer and the poorer, the suppliers and the recipients, can discuss their problems as friendly associates with a common aim. This has disposed them to speak with candor and be less inclined to resent analysis of their deficiencies and suggestions for their correction. It has been made easier for the poorer to secure technical instruction and advice from whichever associate could give it. Each has been enabled to send its students to whatever country within the group made room for them in its schools. Pooled resources have made possible projects that no single participant would have been willing to finance alone. And it has given the providers of aid an acceptable right or title to try and assure themselves that their aid was well and honestly used for the designated purpose.

As a result of activities fostered by the Colombo Plan, the conditions of those countries of South and Southeast Asia which are not active battlegrounds have been bettered a little—a very little—despite their marked growth in population. Their supplies of food and electric power and water have been augmented. A variety of new industries has been brought into existence. Thousands of their young men and women have been trained in the practical sciences of business management and production, in the arts of government administration, in the humane professions such as medicine, public health and law, and have been prepared to be teachers in the schools of their own countries. This is a great deal considering the modest cost.

But, as admitted in the reports of the Consultative Committee of the Plan, only a very small breach has been made in the vicious circle, in this whole region of low production, low income, low saving, and resultant lagging economies. The task has proved to be larger and more arduous and demanding than was foreseen at the time the Colombo Plan was inaugurated in 1951.

The operations of the Colombo Plan have been locally shadowed by the inclinations and actions of Indonesia. The benefits that have accrued to the people of that country from the financial and technical aid given by the United States and the members of the Colombo Plan have been offset by the large diversion of resources for military purposes. The future course of Indonesia may impose such a strain on relations between the members of the Colombo Plan as to lead either to the withdrawal or expulsion of Indonesia.[6] The rejection by Cambodia of American aid and its professions of friendship for Communist China may also affect its future in the organization.

But the greater hindrance to progress has been the determined attempt of Communist China, the Soviet Union and North Vietnam to extend their conquest over the whole Southeastern part of Asia. The former Western colonial powers having been expelled, the burden of giving military and economic support to the small countries imminently threatened—South Vietnam, Laos, Cambodia and Thailand—has mainly fallen upon the United States. Should American efforts fail and these countries fall under Communist domination, the whole Colombo Plan organization would be disrupted.

I doubt whether either the Western guardians of this region or

6. In 1963 the American government reduced its help for Indonesia and the British government stated that while it would continue programs under way, it would not inaugurate new ones.

the Communist seekers of power will be able to do much in the longer run to change the state or ways of these primitively living, fecund and very different peoples. For both will have to contend with the inherited hindrances, the impositions of nature, and the tendency of their numbers to grow as fast as rice grains.

I will not try to condense into a few summary generalizations these many and diverse comments on the relative advantages and risks of channeling foreign aid through national or multinational agencies. Perhaps even this brief review will have indicated that they are so complex and variable that judgment must remain fluid and decision must continue to be flexible—experimental and opportunistic.

Nor will I try to predict the part that the several kinds of multinational agencies may play in future dispensations of aid. My best surmise is that it will be increased, despite the wild and restless movements of nationalism, on the surface and in the depths. Little is to be lost by testing more amply and daringly what these (and other) multinational agencies may be able to do to ameliorate the lot of the poor and improve the disposition of nations toward one another. Their chance fully to show what they can do waits upon the ebbing of the cold war, control of competitive arms expenditure, and greater self-knowledge and self-restraint in national behavior. They may be able to shorten the wait. If these improvements in the conduct of nations do not occur, all political structures—international and national—will, like so many older ones, be ultimately ruined, buried under the soil of centuries.

16 | Reflections on
the Outer Reaches of
the Subject

Policy makers are cast as prophets rather than historians. Students
of their problems and actions ought to emulate them. I have tried
to use reminders from the past to guide surmises about the future.
I have sought to foresee what occurrences, attitudes, and influ-
ences are likely to be dominant during the decade or so ahead—a
relatively short time. That is all. Even as restricted and cautious
an attempt to press the complexities of history into advisory service for the future is likely to be outwitted, or even negated by later
actualities.

As long as the ominous cold war continues, its vicissitudes and
demands will, indeed should, influence our aid programs. Yet most
Americans would be pleased to have the United States go down
in history as a country that strove to help others because it really
wanted to, and not merely because of its own transient political
and economic aims. The habit of taking unto one's self the troubles
of others is apt to grow if means permit and generosity is rewarded, deepening the sense of obligation and willingness to

make contributions. As the aid program proceeded, the American government has looked less for gratitude or unfailing support. It has responded more to the claims improved by evidences of will to self-help and progressive and peaceful disposition. The evolving nature of the association between this country and the recipients of its help has become more flexible and mutually tolerant. I believe this is admirable. But we must reserve the right to expect and ask that any nation to which we give substantial help will not do the United States serious harm; that it will stand with us in any critical issues if it wishes our help in the future.

What the American people are doing—outside of the customary course of trade and migration—is to transfer to poorer countries a small share of their accumulated and potential assets. They are passing on some of their productivity, knowledge and experience. By doing so, they are trying not only to relieve present poverty but also to help recipients to master and permanently transform their natural resources and their political and social environment.

Even though many or most of the impoverished peoples assisted by the United States better themselves notably in, say, the next twenty years, the disparity between the economic level on which they live and the one on which the American people live may become greater not less than it is now, if measured by relative per capita money income. But for true appraisal of what is done, we must look deeper than this facile standard of comparison. Small advances in food supply, diet, housing, education, health, medical care and the chance to forge ahead mean much more in the lives of the very poor than ascent into greater comfort and luxury of those who are well off. I do not belittle the enjoyment that may (or may not) be had from living in a roomy house, having two or more automobiles in the garage, a battery of appliances in the kitchen, original models of *haute couture*, staterooms on world cruises, tickets for $100-a-plate dinners and dances for good or gay causes. Against these more costly pleasures, simpler satisfactions —enough flavorsome food, an airy and dry house, needed medication, warm clothes, a new dress for holidays and anniversaries, a visit to town—do not stack up in monetary terms. But when people who have not had them procure them, they make an enormous difference in their way and length of life. Thus one may anticipate that the disparity in human condition and experience will lessen, although differences in money income may grow greater. Whether, if that occurs, countries emerging from poverty will become more cheerfully hopeful or more envious of the few really affluent, I will not venture to predict.

The chronicles of the past contain many plain tales of how countries that were poor and primitive, vigorous and gifted, having drawn on the resources of a richer one and having absorbed its knowledge, surpassed it. Some have then proceeded to subordinate or subdue their tutors or benefactors.

Such instances—of which there are scores in history—should keep the United States alerted to the chance that it may be nurturing a future rival and/or enemy. But as a general precept, it ought not to compress its efforts to aid others because of fear that might occur.

Numerous nations which the United States is helping have made little or no contribution to the search for enduring peace. They seem to have resigned themselves to the prospect that the cold war will go on forever and the possibility that it may end in mutual extinction. Some among them have felt too weak or too immersed in domestic troubles to try to give a hand to the stronger countries. Others may be influenced by the wish to have this struggle continue, believing it to be more helpful rather than harmful to themselves since it tends to cause all adversaries to pay more attention to their wishes. Still others, because of lingering resentment against Western imperialism, have tended to condone the aggressions and oppressions of Communism. These must, and probably will, learn better and act with more foresight.

Nothing could do more to turn the indifferent or hesitant poor nations into advocates of accords about disputed political issues and arms control than a firm pledge that a fair fraction of the consequent reduction in military expenditures would be devoted to helping them. The United States (and other Western capitalist countries) ought to assure the needier ones that if and when the exigencies of the cold war wane, its economic aid will expand, not shrink.

American judgment is still in flux between brimming and hopeful acceptance of leadership to relieve world poverty and shortsighted and half-hearted repudiation of the obligation. Contrast the flourish with which President Truman proposed the Point IV Program in 1947, and the gusto with which President Kennedy took up the cause in 1961, with the narrowed-down views of our foreign aid program expressed in the Report of the Clay Commission and the critical doubts about the value of the aid activities allocated for them in the current Foreign Assistance Act, which caused Congress so greatly to reduce the amounts provided.

Such changes in the face we show the world scarcely constitute the best way to keep either self-confidence or the confidence of others. They reveal how gusts of impatient idealism or disillusionment, imitative thinking in professional and official circles, propaganda and politics can confuse judgment and twist it about. The American people have had time enough by now to gauge the persistent realities: roughly to know the size of the task; the means for progressing with it, the many obstacles, the unavoidable dilemmas; and the probable quota of disagreeable surprises, wastes and disappointments. They ought no longer to be too elated by sporadic successes, or dejected by sporadic disappointments.

The means and the will exist to make poverty yield to progress. But they will succeed in doing so ultimately only if the stronger and wealthier nations live together in reliable peace; a peace rest-ing on accord and mutual consideration—not merely mutual terror. While we strive to bring this about, our will to help others must be indefatigable—accepting the truth of Francis Bacon's dictum, "In all negotiations of Difficulties, a Man may not look to sowe and reape at once: But must Prepare Business, and so Ripen it by Degrees."

Index